CRANFORD AT CHRISTMAS

CRANFORD AT CHRISTMAS

Based on the Cranford stories by Elizabeth Gaskell

adapted for the stage by Laura Turner

JOSEF WEINBERGER PLAYS

LONDON

CRANFORD AT CHRISTMAS
First published in 2014
by Josef Weinberger Ltd
12-14 Mortimer Street, London W1T 3JJ
www.josef-weinberger.com / plays@jwmail.co.uk

ISBN: 978 0 85676 351 9

Printed by Commercial Colour Press plc, Hainault, Essex

For RWM

CRANFORD AT CHRISTMAS was first performed at the Trinity Arts Centre, Gainsborough on 12th November 2011, produced by Chapterhouse Theatre Company. The cast was as follows:

MISS MATTY JENKYNS	Kirsty Cox
PETER JENKYNS	Mark Middleton
MISS POLE	Grace Miller
MRS JAMIESON	Jenni Lea-Jones
MISS MARY SMITH	Rhia Coles
MAJOR ADAMS	Daniel Horn
MARTHA	Nicky Diss
JEM HEARN	Adam Grayson
LADY GLENMIRE	Nicky Diss
DOCTOR HOGGINS	Kevin Thomas
BETTY	Jenni Lea-Jones
THOMAS	Daniel Horn
MISTLETOE SELLER	Kevin Thomas
MR MULLINER	Adam Grayson
MRS FORRESTER	Nicky Diss
PENNY POST BOY	Daniel Horn
CAROL SINGER	Nicky Diss
VILLAGER	Nicky Diss

Directed by Rebecca Gadsby

Set design by Peter Eldridge

Costumes designed by Georgina Nurse and Pearl Constaqnce

Lighting Designed by Jason Addison and Mark Burman

Original Music by Richard Main

CHARACTERS

Miss Matty Jenkyns

Peter Jenkyns

Miss Pole

Mrs Jamieson

Miss Mary Smith

Major Adams

Martha

Jem Hearn

Lady Glenmire

Doctor Hoggins

Betty

Mr Mulliner

Mrs Forrester

Thomas

Mistletoe Seller

Carol Singer

Penny Post Boy

Villager

SUGGESTED DOUBLINGS

Miss Matty Jenkyns

Miss Pole

Miss Mary Smith

Mrs Jamieson / Betty

Major Adams / Thomas / Penny Post Boy

Lady Glenmire / Martha / Mrs Forrester / Carol Singer / Villager

Peter Jenkyns

Jem Hearn / Mr Mulliner

Doctor Higgins / Mistletoe Seller

FOREWORD

I am indebted to Richard Main at Chapterhouse Theatre Company
for giving me the opportunity to write an original play based
on Elizabeth Gaskell's unforgettable characters and to see it
performed with such a brilliant cast and creative team. Thank
you to everyone involved, most especially Beck Gadsby for her
beautiful direction.

My thanks to Matt Connell, Alex Cory and all at Berlin Associates
as well as all at Weinberger's.

To my mum, dad, my nanna and all my family, thank you for
supporting me and lots of love always. To all my friends but
especially Emily and Nessah, thank you for being there and sorry I
disappear for weeks to write.

Laura Turner, May 2014

ACT ONE

Scene One

Cranford Village Square.

CAROL SINGERS sing a carol. Montage of village life, culminating in a standoff between MISS POLE and the CAROL SINGERS as she tries to barge through them and refuses to put money in their collection tin. As the SINGERS finish, a bell starts to toll the hour ten. Exeunt.

Scene 2

MISS MATTY's teashop / parlour.

A fireplace, a small table surrounded by chairs and a chaise-long sofa. At one side, by the street entrance to the shop, a tall desk with tea caddies and a hand bell. Boxes of Christmas decorations on the floor and table. The room is partly decorated for Christmas. The final chime of ten. Enter MISS MATTY and MARY, tying on aprons.

MISS MATTY	Mary, off with your morning cap!
	(MARY *disposes of her cap. She and* MISS MATTY *rush about, tidying boxes and putting up decorations. Enter* MISS POLE *from upstairs.*)
MISS POLE	I don't know why you must open before calling hours have commenced. Would it be such a burden to prolong opening just until twelve?
MISS MATTY	I may offend propriety by opening outside of the designated calling hours, but I should offend my purse if I did not trade in the

morning. Martha would certainly find the
news troubling.

MISS POLE   What has she got to do with it?

MISS MATTY   Servants are generally most aggrieved when
              you are unable to pay them.

MISS POLE   What of etiquette? There was a time when
              every woman in Cranford abided by strict,
              unspoken rules of conduct. Calling hours,
              twelve till two. Never prolong a visit beyond
              fifteen minutes. Serve sponge fingers, never
              biscuits.

MARY   Yet you are here, Miss Pole.

              (MISS POLE *looks at her sharply.*)

              It is only ten o'clock but you have been
              calling on us for the past forty minutes. And
              you ate a biscuit with your tea.

MISS POLE   It is futile to resist the unstoppable
              advancing of so-called progress. One must
              bring oneself to move with the times.

              (MARY *gathers up the decorations on the
              table.*)

MARY   This shall be the merriest teashop in the
              county.

MISS POLE   I have no taste for this fuss and frippery. I
              loathe the expectation that every Tabitha,
              Dorothy and Harriet must bedeck her house
              with greenery. It is unnatural to invite the
              outside world into one's home.

MARY   You need to get into the festive spirit, Miss
                Pole.

                (MARY *goes to place a sprig of holly in* MISS
                POLE'S *hair. A glare from* MISS POLE *stops
                her.*)

MISS POLE   Christmas is full of potholes. Potholes
                that may cause even the most diligent
                to stumble and falter whilst trying to
                valiantly navigate the customs and rituals
                of the season. Deliver cards by hand or by
                Penny Post? Light a candle for each day of
                advent, or just each week? I do not care at
                all for this suffocating season of sultanas
                and cinnamon. I should not be sorry if
                Christmas simply disappeared in a puff of
                smoke overnight.

MISS MATTY   I do not think there is much chance of Old
                Saint Nick giving up his occupation quite so
                abruptly.

MISS POLE   As for him, there is something deeply
                troubling about the idea of a grossly
                overweight man sneaking into the bedrooms
                of unsuspecting females in the middle of the
                night under the guise of giving them gifts.
                I should like to give that rascal a gift of my
                own!

                (*Enter* MARTHA *with a tray of tea and plate
                of pie.*)

MARTHA   Kettle's on the boil for yer customers, Miss
                Matty ma'am, and I'm puttin' Thomas on
                servin' duty while I go ter store for supplies.

                (MARTHA *hands round tea.*)

MISS MATTY	Such responsibility, Martha?

MARTHA   He knows if he does owt wrong, he'll be gettin' a clout round the ear so I don't think he'll be makin' any careless mistakes. (*To* MISS POLE.) Cinnamon, apple and sultana pie?

MARY   Miss Pole does not like anything to do with cinnamon and sultanas.

(MARTHA *looks affronted and petulantly dumps the plate down. Exit* MARTHA.)

MISS MATTY   She is definitely not herself.

MISS POLE   A smack will help her remember her place. But I suppose I might eat some to ease the dispute.

(MISS POLE *takes some pie.*)

MISS MATTY   I am worried – concerned for her. It's like she has some unpleasant weight playing upon her mind.

MARY   She certainly seems distracted – tired. I heard her snap at Thomas for muddying the kitchen floor twice this week.

MISS MATTY   Should I speak to her? I don't want her to feel pressured to confide in me. I am only her employer.

MARY   You are much more than that to her, just as she is to you.

MISS MATTY   Martha and Jem have been dear friends to me. I am not proud to say it, but I so dread that they may wish to set up home themselves. I know it is the course that newlyweds desire to follow.

MISS POLE   Let serving maids' business remain their own. You see there was no point in opening so early after all. No one has come, and I don't suppose anyone shall until the clock strikes twelve. The sacred statutes of society still hold sway in Cranford.

(*The doorbell rings.*)

MISS MATTY   Quickly, Mary, the calling caps!

(MARY *retrieves the calling caps. She and* MISS MATTY *put them on. Enter* MR MULLINER.)

MR MULLINER   The Honourable Mrs Jamieson.

MISS POLE   Thank heavens it is not a real customer. Mrs Jamieson will certainly not expect to pay for her tea.

(*Enter* MRS JAMIESON *with Peppo the poodle.*)

MRS JAMIESON   Good day, ladies.

MARY   Peppo!

MRS JAMIESON   He cannot abide being left alone. Can you my little poppet? No, you can't, you can't, can you?

(MRS JAMIESON *sits. Peppo takes an interest in the pile of decorations.*)

Peppo, no! Come away from those things!

(MARY *tries to play with Peppo. She ties
some tinsel around his neck. He looks taken
aback.*)

MISS MATTY   We are decorating the shop for Christmas.

MRS JAMIESON   How . . . cosmopolitan.

                  (*She notices Peppo.*)

                  Miss Smith, Peppo is not doll upon which
                  you may enact your every whim!

MARY   I didn't mean –

MRS JAMIESON   You think, I suppose, that just because he
                  is not gifted with human speech that he is
                  not an intelligent, thinking creature. We
                  cannot abide people who treat animals like
                  ignorant little babies. Can we my little
                  coochiepoochiepoo? No we can't, we can't,
                  can we?

MARY   I did not mean to offend you, Mrs Jamieson.

MRS JAMIESON   It is not I you have offended. You do not
                  need to apologise to *me*.

                  (*Beat. Peppo looks at* MARY *expectantly.*)

MARY   I'm sorry . . . Peppo.

MRS JAMIESON   He can detect any sign of reticence in your
                  voice, you know.

MARY   I hope you might find it in your heart to
                  forgive me, Peppo.

                  (MRS JAMIESON *consults Peppo.*)

MRS JAMIESON   He is satisfied with your humility.

MARY   Perhaps I should remove the offending article –

(MARY *goes to remove the tinsel. Peppo retreats.*)

MRS JAMIESON   Peppo is most sensitive to invasions of his personal space.

(MRS JAMIESON *tries to remove the tinsel but Peppo withdraws.*)

Peppo, do not be obtuse.

(*She tries again. Peppo withdraws further.*)

Peppo, do not make me raise my voice!

(*She tries again. Peppo cowers.*)

You are displeasing Mama greatly. I do not wish to fall out with you!

(*Peppo hides.*)

(*To the* WOMEN.) Excuse me.

(MRS JAMIESON *conducts a whispered conference with Peppo that culminates in her removing the tinsel. She turns back to the group.*)

We have reached an accord. I presume you are still in the habit of serving tea in your teashop, Miss Matilda?

(MISS MATTY *realises what* MRS JAMIESON *means. She goes to the tea caddies.*)

MISS MATTY	I have lately received some very fine Oolong. The champagne of teas, they call it!
MRS JAMIESON	Clearly *they* – whoever they may be – have never sampled a fine English Earl Grey. Upstanding and dependable, just as a proper English gentleman should be. Isn't that right, Mulliner?
MR MULLINER	Quite, my lady.
MARY	But it doesn't actually come from England?
MRS JAMIESON	Why would you say such a thing? I would certainly know if it were from some foreign place. I have no taste whatsoever for exotic cuisine.

(*Enter* THOMAS.)

THOMAS	Miss Matty ma'am! I'm sorry ma'am but I just run all the way from the village square. Everyone's talkin' about it, ma'am!
MISS POLE	About what?
THOMAS	The village Christmas party, ma'am, it's in – what were the word? Peril!
MISS POLE	How so?
THOMAS	It's the Assembly Rooms, there's an infestation!
MISS MATTY	Infestation?
MRS JAMIESON	Not . . . mice?
THOMAS	Woodlice!

MARY   Woodlice?

THOMAS   Pourin' outta the windows, miss, and
                scuttlin' all down the steps into the village
                square!

MISS POLE   An invasion.

THOMAS   They're gettin' a man in, but the party, it's
                gonna have ter be cancelled!

MISS MATTY   But it's a tradition!

MISS POLE   Christmas in Cranford would not be the
                same without it.

MRS JAMIESON   Ladies, the solution is simple. A new venue
                must be found.

MISS POLE   But it would need to cater to the specific
                requirements of the concert. Room enough
                for the carol singers to perform and the
                dancing that follows; seating for guests; a
                generous supply of tea . . .

                (*They all look at* MISS MATTY.)

MISS MATTY   Those qualities would certainly be
                necessary.

                (*She realises what* MISS POLE *is suggesting.*)

                Oh!

MARY   Say you will, Miss Matty!

MISS MATTY   I am no party hostess.

MRS JAMIESON   You are hosting a gathering now. It is
                practically the same thing.

MISS MATTY	I – I would need more tables, more chairs, more tea!
MISS POLE	We can easily come by those things.
MRS JAMIESON	It is decided. Mulliner, the sedan.

(*Exit* MR MULLINER.)

Miss Pole, you are an enthusiastic disseminator of information. You might travel with me to impart the happy news.

MISS POLE	I should be delighted.

(*Exit* MRS JAMIESON *with Peppo*.)

This is an honour indeed, Miss Matty. You must do the party justice, or Mrs Jamieson will be most displeased.

(*Exit* MISS POLE. MISS MATTY *sits down in shock*.)

THOMAS	What shall I do now, Miss Matty ma'am?
MISS MATTY	I think you had better order some more tea.

(*Blackout*.)

Scene Three

Outside MISS MATTY *and* MISS POLE's *houses*.

Enter MISS POLE *with a wreath. She holds it up against her house, trying it at different angles. Enter* MISTLETOE SELLER.

SELLER	Mistletoe for yer hallway, ma'am?

MISS POLE	Do I look like I would have any use for that insidious weed? I suggest you take it elsewhere.
	(*Enter* MARTHA, *with a shopping basket.* MISS POLE *observes, unnoticed.*)
JEM	(*off stage*) Martha! Martha!
SELLER	(*to* MARTHA) Mistletoe ter charm yer beau, miss?
MARTHA	Not now, thank yer.
	(*Enter* JEM.)
SELLER	(*to* JEM) Mistletoe for yer missus, sir?
JEM	Not now. Martha, I were callin' yer.
MARTHA	Thought yer were at work.
JEM	Saw yer pass the workshop.
MARTHA	Just goin' ter the store.
JEM	Did yer talk ter her this morning?
MARTHA	Be sellin' out o' spices if I don't hurry. I said ter Miss Matty, I were sure we had plenty o' nutmeg left but the pot were empty when I went ter make a pudding this mornin'. Tell yer what, I'll use some o' my wages, buy some extra and make a puddin' for yer and all.
JEM	Martha –
MARTHA	Back ter work with yer or we won't have any money for no puddings!

(MARTHA *kisses* JEM. MISS POLE *averts her eyes. As* MARTHA *turns to go,* JEM *grabs her.*)

JEM   Have yer told her, lass?

MARTHA   Let go, yer great oaf!

JEM   Have yer spoken ter Miss Matty?

MARTHA   Jem, yer hurtin' me!

JEM   Have yer?

MARTHA   No!

JEM   Why not?

MARTHA   Mind yer own why not! (*Beat.*) Scared, ain't I?

JEM   I ain't meanin' ter upset yer, but yer my wife and I've gotta at least try and take yer in hand!

MARTHA   Yer can take this in hand and all yer great donkey!

                (MARTHA *goes to whack* JEM, *but he catches her arm.*)

JEM   This ain't gonna go away, lass. Yer've gotta face up ter it, and yer've gotta tell Miss Matty. For her own good. Sooner rather than later and all. 'Fore it's too late.

SELLER   Lovers' remedy?

MARTHA & JEM   Not now!

(*Exit* SELLER. MARTHA *starts to cry.* JEM
holds her, gives her his handkerchief. Exit
JEM. MARTHA *wipes her face and turns to*
go. MISS POLE *looks for somewhere to hide.*
In desperation, she holds the wreath up to
mask her face.)

MARTHA   How do yer do, Miss Pole.

(*Exit* MARTHA. MISS POLE *hurries to* MISS
MATTY'S *house and knocks on the window.*
The window opens and MISS MATTY *appears.*)

MISS POLE   Do you have a hammer, Matty dear?

MISS MATTY   A hammer?

MISS POLE   I have made a wreath –

MISS MATTY   But you were so opposed to festive
                    embellishments?

MISS POLE   It is a fine thing I chose today to adjust my
                    opinion, as I have just witnessed your maid
                    getting up to all sorts of mischief. Kissing.
                    The carpenter.

(Enter PETER JENKYNS *and* MAJOR ADAMS,
unseen by MISS MATTY *and* MISS POLE. *They*
carry bags and consult a map.)

MISS POLE   He is her husband.

MISS POLE   Kissing one moment, at odds the next.

MISS MATTY   At odds?

MISS POLE   Arguing about something or other.

MISS MATTY   Was it serious?

MISS POLE	Miss Matty, I have much better things to do than eavesdrop on juveniles who choose to cavort in the street! Do you have a hammer or must I trouble myself to go to Mr Johnson?

MISS MATTY   Jem is sure to have one in his workshop. I shall send Thomas.

(MISS MATTY *starts to retreat.* MISS POLE *notices the* MEN.)

MISS POLE   (*sotto*) Miss Matty, wait! Do not be alarmed, but there are two members of the inferior sex conversing over there.

(MISS MATTY *leans out of the window and sees them in horror.*)

MISS MATTY   Then I must withdraw before they catch sight of us whispering across the window ledge!

MISS POLE   What about me?

MISS MATTY   Hasten home.

MISS POLE   But there is no possibility of passing them without being observed! I throw myself upon your mercy, Miss Matty! I beg you – let me in!

MISS MATTY   Through the window?

MISS POLE   You would not leave me out here to fend for myself alone?

(MISS POLE *scrabbles at the window frame as* MISS MATTY *tries to close the window.*

PETER *and* MAJOR ADAMS *notice the commotion.*)

MAJOR ADAMS   Good day!

(MISS POLE *and* MISS MATTY *freeze. Beat.*)

MISS MATTY   Good day, sir.

(MISS POLE *remains paralysed.*)

MAJOR ADAMS   I wonder if you might direct me towards the lodgings of a Mrs Forrester?

MISS MATTY   You are very near. Continue up the street – her house is in the square opposite the Lamb and Flag public house.

MAJOR ADAMS   Most obliged, madam.

(*Exeunt* PETER *and* MAJOR ADAMS.)

MISS POLE   Imagine! Addressing someone through their window!

MISS MATTY   Do you think they were strangers?

MISS POLE   They must certainly be strangers to be arriving to stay with Mrs Forrester so close to Christmas. She does not have a soul left in the world who would come to spend the season with her. But to think she is now taking in lodgers! A woman, living alone and granting houseroom to two gentlemen – *if* they be gentlemen! Frailty, thy name is man. Remember that, Miss Matty, the next time you decide to converse with men folk through your window!

(MISS MATTY *closes her window on an
affronted* MISS POLE. *Blackout.*)

Scene Four

MISS MATTY'S *teashop / parlour.*

MISS MATTY *is looking through a box of decorations. She
withdraws one, then looks at the cameo she wears.*

MISS MATTY   Matilda Jenkyns. Reverend's daughter.
                  Teashop proprietor. Village Christmas
                  party hostess. (*Beat.*) I long to be the kind
                  of person who can step in and save the
                  day, rescue the party, but I am not made
                  for these sorts of entertainments. My dear
                  sister – you, Deborah, you of all know
                  how I struggle with such gatherings. And
                  at Christmas. It is a celebration, but it is
                  also a time of quiet contemplation, solemn
                  reflection.

MISS POLE   (*off stage*) Out of my way! Out of my way!

                  (MISS MATTY *replaces the cameo and
                  decoration. Enter* MARY, *directing* JEM *and*
                  THOMAS, *barely visible behind the Christmas
                  tree they carry.*)

MARY   Left a bit! No, right a bit! A bit more. Left a
                  bit!

MISS MATTY   (*to* MISS POLE) Thomas, would you fetch
                  my apron? Opening hours are almost upon
                  us and we expect Mrs Jamieson and Mrs
                  Forrester shortly.

(*Enter* MISS POLE, *holding Christmas cards.*
She stops short with horror when she sees
JEM *setting up the tree. Exit* THOMAS.)

MARY   Miss Pole, are they Christmas cards?

MISS POLE   Haven't you written yours yet, girl?

MARY   I thought you were quite against Christmas?

MISS POLE   Sending Christmas cards has nothing to do
                with Christmas! It is a social obligation.

                (MARY *goes to help* JEM *decide which side*
                of the tree should face front. Enter THOMAS
                with MISS MATTY'S *apron. She goes to put it*
                on but sees a large green stain.)

THOMAS   I'm sorry, ma'am. I – I spilt some tea on it.

MISS POLE   Tea.

THOMAS   Green . . . tea.

MISS POLE   Lying is a very odious offence, boy. Green
                tea indeed.

MISS MATTY   Thomas? You shall not be in trouble.

THOMAS   Spilt me supper on the kitchen table t'other
                night, ma'am. Just grabbed the first thing I
                saw ter mop it up.

MISS MATTY   Your supper?

THOMAS   Pea soup. I didn't want Martha ter shout at
                me again for messin' up her kitchen. I'm
                sorry I ruined yer apron, ma'am.

MISS MATTY	Thank you for telling me the truth. I'm sure Martha has lots for you to do.
	(*Exit* THOMAS.)
	Mary, we shall have to make that material order this afternoon.
MISS POLE	You can buy new aprons quite easily, I assure you. You need not make them yourself.
MISS MATTY	I think I am quite through with aprons. I intend to make myself a uniform instead.
MISS POLE	A uniform?
MISS MATTY	It will be practical, preserve my dresses and mark me as the owner of a respectable teashop.
MISS POLE	It will mark you as a social outcast! (*Beat.*) Matty dear, it is enough to be a member of the serving profession without advertising the fact every time you are seen about the village!
MISS MATTY	I envisaged it in navy. I thought it might be rather chic.
MISS POLE	Navy? Chic?
MARY	Miss Pole, why don't you help me decorate the tree?
MISS POLE	That monstrous thing?
MISS MATTY	I think there must still be some boxes upstairs. I bought some very pretty baubles

last Christmas, they don't seem to be
anywhere.

MARY   Let's have a look.

                (MISS MATTY *starts to go.*)

MISS POLE   Do not leave me with that beastly bush!

                (*Exeunt* MISS MATTY *and* MISS POLE. MARY
                starts to follow them.)

JEM   Can I have a word, ma'am?

MARY   Jem? What's troubling you?

JEM   It's not so much troublin' me, ma'am, but
                see it's . . . it's Martha. Has she spoken
                with yer, with Miss Matty, about . . . about
                anythin' just lately?

MARY   I don't think so. Not to me.

JEM   I see. Thank yer, Miss Smith. I ain't meanin'
                ter be troublin' yer with my awkwardness
                and questions.

MARY   Martha is well, isn't she?

JEM   There's nowt for yer ter fear, Miss Smith.
                I'll be on my way, leave yer ter decorate
                yer tree. It's a fine one that. Right fit for a
                mistress like Miss Matty.

                (*Exit* JEM. *Enter* MISS POLE, *carrying a box.*)

MISS POLE   I see you are trying to evade the heavy
                lifting.

(*Exit* MARY. MISS POLE *puts her box on the floor and bends over to look through. Enter* PETER JENKYNS.)

PETER   Good day, madam –

                 (MISS POLE *jumps and turns to see* PETER.)

                 I did not mean to startle you.

MISS POLE   You cannot fright me so easily, sir. You might sit down if you please.

                 (PETER *sits and watches* MISS POLE *as she returns to the box*.)

PETER   You look quite different to how I imagined you might.

MISS POLE   I beg your pardon?

PETER   It has long been my desire to return to Cranford. To see you.

MISS POLE   Return to Cranford?

PETER   I so hoped you would still be here to answer the deepest desire of my heart.

MISS POLE   Control yourself, sir!

PETER   You – you do not recognise me?

MISS POLE   I have never seen you before in my life.

PETER   I thought . . . surely I do not look so very different?

                 (PETER *tries to take* MISS POLE'S *hand but she snatches it away*.)

MISS POLE   You insult decorum!

PETER   Might we at least have a cup of tea together?

MISS POLE   I think not. Besides, I have nothing to do with the dunking of leaves or the boiling of kettles.

PETER   Yet you possess a teashop?

(*Beat.* MISS POLE *is affronted.*)

MISS POLE   Do I look like a teashop owner?

PETER   I'm sorry?

MISS POLE   I have some aura of the shopkeeper about my person?

PETER   I am not well acquainted with shopkeepers in general. Perhaps I should leave you to your business.

MISS POLE   My business of looking like a shopkeeper?

MISS MATTY   (*off stage*) Careful, Mary! Careful!

PETER   This is Miss Matilda Jenkyns' teashop?

MISS POLE   Do not play the innocent with me!

(*Enter* MARY, *carrying boxes piled high in front of her face.*)

MARY   Miss Pole?

(MISS POLE *glares at* PETER *and goes to help* MARY. PETER *slips away. Exit* PETER.)

MISS POLE	(*to* PETER) Though I would not have accepted your help, it is very unchivalrous of you not to offer assistance to two ladies.
MARY	Who are you talking to?
	(MISS POLE *and* MARY *put the boxes down.* MISS POLE *looks around.*)
MISS POLE	He's gone!
MARY	Who's gone?
MISS POLE	That man!
MARY	What man?
MISS POLE	The one sitting there!
MARY	Where?
MISS POLE	That is just like a man to disappear precisely when you need him.
MARY	Maybe it was your friend Saint Nick.
	(MISS POLE *is scornful.*)
	Maybe it was a ghost.
MISS POLE	There is no such thing.
	(MARY *sorts through some decorations.* MISS POLE *glances about suspiciously, checking under the sofa for ghosts. Enter* MISS MATTY *in a clean apron.*)
MISS MATTY	They are a lost cause.

MISS POLE	Miss Matty, you must purchase material to make yourself a uniform as soon as possible so you may be correctly identified as the proprietress of this establishment and thereby rescue innocent bystanders from the unwelcome burden of misidentification.
MISS MATTY	I shall make the necessary enquiries as you are now so in favour of the idea.

(*Enter* THOMAS.)

Thomas, I said sit at the kitchen window to watch for Mrs Jamieson's sedan.

THOMAS	If yer mean the snooty-nosed dog lady, she's at the door now, ma'am.
MISS POLE	Impertinent boy!
THOMAS	Beggin' yer pardon, ma'am, but I were just abidin' by what yer said 'bout tellin' the truth, so that were all I meant when I said she had a snooty-nose 'cos she does have a snooty-nose and she's got a dog with her or at least I think it were a dog but it might've been a rat but whatever it were I didn't mean to offend no one.
MISS MATTY	Go and see if we have any sponge fingers.
THOMAS	There ain't none, ma'am.
MISS MATTY	How could you possibly know that without looking?
THOMAS	'Cos I ate the last one this mornin'.
MISS POLE	(*to* MISS MATTY) You won't stand for that?

THOMAS   I were only –

MISS MATTY   Telling the truth, I know. Is there anything
                  in the kitchen to serve?

THOMAS   Some o' them smelly biscuits left.

                  (MISS MATTY *nods. Exit* THOMAS.)

MISS POLE   What a humiliation to inflict upon you.
                  Forcing you to serve biscuits to Mrs
                  Jamieson.

MARY   Take comfort. You may distribute your
                  Christmas cards.

                  (*Enter* MR MULLINER.)

MR MULLINER   The Honourable Mrs Jamieson.

                  (MISS POLE *gets her Christmas cards ready.*
                  Enter MRS JAMIESON *and Peppo. She sees the*
                  tree.)

MRS JAMIESON   Not you as well. Everyone is succumbing to
                  these outlandish new fads.

                  (*Enter* THOMAS, *with a rattling tea tray.*)

MISS MATTY   I like to support progression.

MRS JAMIESON   Progress is a very untrustworthy thing. One
                  can never be entirely confident of where one
                  might end up progressing to. Someone will
                  attempt to inflict a Christmas card on me
                  next, I don't suppose.

                  (MISS POLE *hides her cards.*)

                  Biscuits. How . . . quaint.

MARY   Dandelion flower.

MRS JAMIESON   They remind one terribly of scented soap. I
                am in the mood for sponge fingers. What a
                pity you have none. How fortunate I come
                bearing news as there is so little else on
                offer.

                (MRS JAMIESON *notices* THOMAS.)

                What is he doing hovering about like a
                hornet?

THOMAS   'Scuse me, Miss Matty ma'am, there's
                another lady at the door. She's got some
                kind of cat or ferret or some such wild
                animal on her shoulder, miss.

MISS MATTY   It must be Mrs Forrester and that is a cat.
                Show her in.

                (*Exit* THOMAS.)

MRS JAMIESON   Wild animal was quite correct if it is Mrs
                Forrester with that Pussy-Wilkins of hers.

                (*Peppo tries to hide.*)

                Babushka! Don't fret so!

                (*Peppo and* MRS JAMIESON *hold a brief
                conference.*)

                Mulliner. It is time.

                (MR MULLINER *reaches into his jacket.*)

MARY   Would Peppo like some milk, Mrs
                Jamieson?

MRS JAMIESON   He drinks only the finest French cream.
                Served precisely at body temperature.

                (MR MULLINER *presents a small bottle of*
                milk. MRS JAMIESON *feeds Peppo like a baby.*)

MRS JAMIESON   This will calm him. He might even sleep
                through Pussy-Wilkins' visit. Peppo always
                likes a little snooze after a feed, don't you,
                my little coochiewoo? I can't understand
                why you let that wretched creature come
                here.

MARY   I thought you were an animal lover, Mrs
                Jamieson.

MRS JAMIESON   I am. I was talking about Mrs Forrester.

                (*Enter* THOMAS *and* MRS FORRESTER *with*
                Pussy-Wilkins.)

MRS FORRESTER   (*very loudly*) Oh, hello!

                (MRS JAMIESON *winces. Peppo cowers.*)

MRS FORRESTER   Mrs Jamieson! Peppo!

MRS JAMIESON   (*coldly*) Mrs Forrester. Pussy-Wilkins.

MARY   Hello, Pussy-Wilkins! (*To* MRS FORRESTER.)
                Would you like tea?

MRS FORRESTER   He most certainly does not have fleas!

                (MRS FORRESTER *converses with* MISS MATTY
                and MISS POLE *as her tea is poured.*)

MRS JAMIESON   Mulliner. Make haste.

(MR MULLINER *withdraws two earplugs and
gives them to* MRS JAMIESON. *She passes
Peppo to him to continue feeding and sees*
MARY *watching her curiously. She shows
her the plugs.*)

MRS JAMIESON   Protection.

MARY   For your ears?

MRS JAMIESON   My sanity.

                (MRS JAMIESON *inserts the plugs. She is
                oblivious to all that proceeds.*)

MRS FORRESTER   Biscuits!

                (MARY *starts tickling Pussy-Wilkins with a
                piece of tinsel.*)

MISS MATTY   Dandelion flower.

MRS FORRESTER   I shall not devour them all! Not when we
                have this –

                (*She produces a bottle of cherry brandy
                from a brown paper bag.*)

                Homemade cherry brandy. A little tipple to
                toast the season!

MISS MATTY   That is very kind, but we must decline.

MRS FORRESTER   It is much nicer than wine! You will have
                some, won't you, Mrs Jamieson? Mrs
                Jamieson?

MRS JAMIESON   Oh, yes.

                (MRS FORRESTER *pours generous measures.*)

MISS POLE   I have never seen such an offensively brash-coloured substance in my life. As though it came straight from hell itself.

MISS MATTY   Is this *very* improper in the middle of the day?

MARY   I once read that the queen has a glass of brandy after luncheon.

MISS MATTY   If royalty do it, there cannot be too much shame in it.

                 (*The* WOMEN *take a glass each.*)

MRS FORRESTER   Chin, chin!

                 (MRS FORRESTER *knocks back her brandy.* MISS POLE, MISS MATTY *and* MARY *take a sip, then cough and splutter.* MRS JAMIESON *takes a tentative sip, then another and another.*)

MISS MATTY   It is very strong.

MISS POLE   I do believe there's spirit in it.

MARY   I didn't know cherries could be so potent.

MISS MATTY   I often feel tipsy from eating damson tart.

MISS POLE   Don't you find it most unpleasant, Mrs Jamieson?

                 (MISS POLE *pokes* MRS JAMIESON *to get her attention.*)

MRS JAMIESON   Oh, yes.

(MRS JAMIESON *continues to drink.* MISS POLE *takes another sip.*)

MISS POLE Ghastly stuff.

(MISS POLE *has another sip.* MRS FORRESTER *tops up* MISS MATTY *and* MARY'S *glasses despite their protestations.*)

MRS FORRESTER More, Mrs Jamieson?

MRS JAMIESON Oh, yes.

(MRS FORRESTER *tops up* MRS JAMIESON'S *glass and her own.* MRS JAMIESON *continues to drink, yawning, her eyes growing heavy.*)

MISS POLE I shall partake of another glass. Just to ensure Mrs Jamieson does not feel embarrassed to be drinking alone.

(MISS POLE *holds out her glass for a refill. She drinks throughout the following.*)

MISS MATTY Mrs Forrester, how are the gentlemen staying with you?

MRS FORRESTER Hmmm?

MISS MATTY How are the gentlemen residing with you?

MISS POLE What is the use? She will never hear.

MARY Mrs Jamieson has fallen asleep!

MRS FORRESTER What was that?

MARY Nothing.

MRS FORRESTER   Beijing? It's funny you should mention
                that place, you know. I have two gentlemen
                lodging with me at the moment – did you
                know? – and one of them claims to have
                been to Cranford before, but they have both
                lately been in Beijing. Or was it Berlin?

MISS MATTY   Been in Cranford before?

MRS FORRESTER   Birmingham!

MISS POLE   Please, Mrs Forrester, Mrs Jamieson is fast
                asleep!

MRS FORRESTER   I very much doubt that Mrs Jamieson's dress
                is cheap. Barcelona!

MISS POLE   (*to* MISS MATTY) You should be most
                gratified that Mrs Jamieson feels so at home
                in your dwelling.

MISS MATTY   I should?

MISS POLE   She could not have paid you a greater
                compliment. Let us hope Mrs Forrester does
                not disrupt her.

MRS FORRESTER   Bruges!

                (MISS MATTY, MISS POLE *and* MARY *shush*
                MRS FORRESTER.)

                Brazil!

MISS POLE   Brazil?

MRS FORRESTER   You'd like a refill?

                (MRS FORRESTER *cheerfully refills* MISS POLE'S
                glass. During the following, MRS JAMIESON

*slumps gradually to the side in her sleep,
her glass tilting dangerously.)*

MRS FORRESTER   Burnley!

MISS POLE   We must be silent and hope she follows suit.

(*Beat.* MISS POLE *hiccups.*)

I – (*She hiccups.*) I cannot control it!

(*She hiccups.* MRS JAMIESON *stirs.*)

Help me!

(*She hiccups.* MRS JAMIESON *settles back to
sleep, tilting to the side dangerously.* MR
MULLINER *tries to prop her up.* MISS POLE
continues to hiccup.)

MARY   Sip a glass of water from the wrong side of a
cup – no, hold your breath for two minutes!

MISS POLE   I am not a fish, Miss Smith!

MISS MATTY   I believe sugar can cure hiccups.

(MISS POLE *eats a spoonful of sugar from the
table.*)

I meant in some tea.

(*Beat.* MISS POLE *hiccups.*)

MARY   Cover your ears.

MISS POLE   They are not that loud!

MARY   You! It is a remedy.

MISS MATTY	I don't think I can cope with any else's hearing being impaired.
MARY	Hold your tongue!
MISS POLE	Don't be so disrespectful!

(MARY *sticks her tongue out and pinches it to demonstrate.*)

| MISS POLE | Put that away! Tongues are not to be seen in teashops. |

(MARY *sees the brown paper bag.*)

MARY	Put this over your mouth.
MISS POLE	Miss Matty, she's trying to asphyxiate me!
MISS MATTY	This is a proven remedy.

(MISS POLE *dubiously puts the bag over her mouth and breathes in and out. During the following, she continues, losing puff with each exhalation. Beat.* MISS MATTY *and* MARY *relish the silence. Pussy-Wilkins gags. Beat. Pussy-Wilkins gags again.*)

| MISS MATTY | Pussy-Wilkins? |

(MRS FORRESTER *realises Pussy-Wilkins is choking. She jumps up, startling Peppo who leaps out of* MR MULLINER's *arms.*)

| MARY | Peppo! |
| MRS FORRESTER | Pussy-Wilkins! |

(MR MULLINER *dives to rescue Peppo as* MISS POLE *faints and collapses against* MRS

JAMIESON, *who awakens with a start, her glass jerking and splashing brandy in* MR MULLINER'S *face as he struggles to his knees beside her chair, Peppo in his arms.*)

MARY   Miss Pole!

(MARY *and* MISS MATTY *rush to* MISS POLE.)

MRS JAMIESON   Mulliner!

(MRS JAMIESON *snatches Peppo.*)

MRS FORRESTER   Pussy-Wilkins! Stop that nasty choking!

(MISS POLE *revives as* MR MULLINER *tries to take Pussy-Wilkins from* MRS FORRESTER. *She resists so he seizes them both and administers the Heimlich manoeuvre. After two attempts, a piece of tinsel flies through the air. Beat.*)

MRS JAMIESON   Clearly I should be grateful I have kept my news to myself until now. I *had* come to inform you that my sister-in-law, Lady Glenmire, is coming to stay. She is a member of the peerage, you know. We shall have many important people to see. After today, I do not suppose you shall see us for the duration of her visit.

MISS POLE   Mrs Jamieson, forgive us for waking you –

MRS JAMIESON   I was not asleep. It is uncommonly bright in here – so bright that I was prevailed upon to close my eyes against the blaze. Mulliner, the sedan.

(*Exeunt* MR MULLINER, MRS JAMIESON *and Peppo.*)

MARY   At least the shock cured your hiccups, Miss
                  Pole.

                  (*Beat.* MISS POLE *hiccups. She sobs and runs
                  off. Exit* MISS POLE. *Beat.*)

MISS MATTY   Tea?

MARY   I'll fetch the Earl Grey.

MRS FORRESTER   Bombay! I knew it began with a B!

                  (*Blackout.*)

Scene Five

Outside MISS MATTY *and* MISS POLE'S *houses.*

Enter MISS POLE. *She stops in her tracks when she sees the
wreath is missing from her house. She looks for it, then
marches to* MISS MATTY'S *house and knocks on the window.
The window opens and* MARY *appears.*

MISS POLE   A most heinous offence has been committed.
                 I have been targeted. I am the victim of a
                 most reprehensible act of criminality. Do
                 not be distressed, but there is a wreath thief
                 at work.

MARY   A what?

MISS POLE   A wreath thief! A garland bandit! A burglar,
                 Miss Smith!

MARY   A robbery?

                 (MISS MATTY *appears at the window.*)

MISS MATTY   Who has been robbed? Miss Pole! Was it
                  anything of worth?

MARY   Just a Christmas wreath.

MISS POLE   You say that with very little respect for
                  the two afternoons' work I invested in that
                  festoon, Miss Smith.

MARY   Perhaps you should alert the constable?

MISS MATTY   You cannot summon the police about a
                  missing wreath.

MISS POLE   Stolen! But I shall not. The police may be
                  the protectors of the realm, but Cranford is
                  a principality that has very little to do with
                  the jurisdiction of men. I shall conduct my
                  own investigations.

                  (*Exit* MISS POLE. *Enter* MARTHA *and* JEM.
                  MISS MATTY *goes to close the window.*)

MARY   It's Martha – and Jem.

MISS MATTY   Come inside. An open window may appear
                  as an invitation to an opportunist burglar.

MARY   But wouldn't it be reassuring to know that
                  everything is as it should be?

MISS MATTY   You are not suggesting I spy on my own
                  maid?

MARY   Not spy! Dispel your fears.

MISS MATTY   I have been worried about her, I confess. A
                  moment of indecision. No, it is wrong. We
                  must allow them their privacy.

MARTHA   D'yer think Miss Matty's noticed?

                    (MISS MATTY *freezes.*)

JEM   Don't know how she could miss it.

                    (MISS POLE'S *window opens and* MISS POLE
                    appears.)

MISS POLE   Miss Matty –

                    (MISS MATTY *and* MARY *shush* MISS POLE.
                    They all watch.)

JEM   But no one's said owt?

MARTHA   Folk could balloon up or shrink down,
                    but even if it were noticed, it wouldn't be
                    spoken of, would it? But I will tell her. Soon
                    as I'm ready.

JEM   Yer been sayin' that for nigh six months.

MARTHA   Jem, don't –

JEM   It's only 'cos – 'cos I'm proud as punch,
                    lass.

MARTHA   Really?

                    (MARTHA *kisses* JEM. *The* WOMEN *avert their
                    eyes.* MISS MATTY *goes to close the window.*)

JEM   Just make sure yer give her notice before
                    baby comes, or yer'll give her a funny turn.

MARTHA   She ain't that old, yer plum pudding!

                    (*Exeunt* MARTHA *and* JEM. *The women stare
                    after them in shock.*)

MISS MATTY   Mary? Did I hear correctly?

MISS POLE   Kissing in the street again!

MISS MATTY   Martha is expecting?

MISS POLE   Expecting a smack I shouldn't hope for
                 speaking about her mistress in that manner.
                 Not that old, indeed!

MARY   She is pregnant.

MISS POLE   With a baby?

MARY   That is usual.

MISS POLE   But she is a servant! I thought this town
                 could descend no further into the mire.
                 Babies, burglaries – who knows what felony
                 will be next?

                 (MISS POLE *retreats inside and slams her
                 window.*)

MISS MATTY   Mary, there is to be a baby in the house! I
                 think there was a pattern for a christening
                 gown in the knitting catalogue!

                 (MARY *and* MISS MATTY *disappear inside
                 and shut the window. Blackout. End of Act
                 One.*)

ACT TWO

Scene One

MISS MATTY'S *teashop / parlour.*

Enter MISS POLE, MARY *and* MISS MATTY.

MISS POLE	I don't know about you, but I did not catch one glimpse of the vulgar and ostentatious lady.
MARY	Mrs Jamieson?
MISS POLE	Lady Glenmire!
MISS MATTY	Mrs Jamieson whisked her through the village very quickly.
MISS POLE	Doubtless they will have a very gloomy, snobbish time together. It is tiresome how Mrs Jamieson clings to her feeble association with the peerage. Lady Glenmire is in reality very little to her now both their husbands are dead.
MARY	What if I see Lady Glenmire in the street? How should I address her?
MISS POLE	Ladies are not to be found rambling about the streets!
MISS MATTY	Should we say "Your Ladyship" where we would say "you" to a common person? It sounds very strange.
MISS POLE	Only because you are not used to it.
MARY	We should practise so we do not feel foolish saying "Your Ladyship" for the first time to

Lady Glenmire herself. What do you think,
Your Ladyship?

MISS MATTY   Mary, you sound so genteel!

MARY   Try it.

MISS MATTY   Tea, Your Ladyship?

MARY   You see? It's quite easy!

MISS POLE   Sponge finger, Your Ladyship? No, ladies do
              not eat sponge fingers. Cucumber sandwich,
              Your Ladyship?

MARY   (*to* MISS POLE) Your Ladyship, would you
              be so kind as to assist in compiling a list of
              items we require for the party?

              (MARY *finds a pen and paper.*)

MISS POLE   Of course, Your Ladyship. A constant
              supply of mince pies and plum pudding are
              necessary, then tea of course and wassail
              punch for the carollers. Do you – does Your
              Ladyship think Mrs Jamieson will still
              come?

MARY   I'm sure she will if we tempt her and Peppo
              with sugarplums.

MISS MATTY   We must get crackers, and purchase
              extra coal for the fire and more candles,
              I suppose. We cannot keep blind man's
              holiday when we have guests. See how much
              is left in the money tin.

MARY   I remember my mother had an ingenious
              scheme for melting the leftover ends of used

                        candles and re-setting the wax to make new
                        ones.

MISS MATTY   A very elegant economy.

MARY   (*to* MISS MATTY) Then let us see what we can
                find, Your Ladyship.

                (*Exeunt* MARY *and* MISS MATTY. MISS POLE
                *withdraws her red enveloped Christmas
                cards from her purse and goes to the fire.
                Enter* PETER *and* MAJOR ADAMS, *unnoticed by*
                MISS POLE, *who prepares to throw her cards
                on the fire.* PETER *rings the hand bell.* MISS
                POLE *jumps guiltily.*)

MISS POLE   Yes, Your Ladyship?

                (MISS POLE *turns and sees* PETER.)

PETER   Not quite, I'm afraid.

                (*A cacophony of thuds and thumps. Candles
                roll into the room. Enter* MARY, *chasing
                the candles.* MISS POLE *conceals her cards.*
                MAJOR ADAMS *bends to pick up a candle at
                the same moment* MARY *reaches for it. They
                almost collide, their eyes meeting.* MAJOR
                ADAMS *picks up the candle and hands it to
                her.*)

MARY   Thank you, sir.

MAJOR ADAMS   So many candles. Are you plotting a séance?
                What have we stumbled into?

MISS POLE   Merely party preparations.

                (*Enter* MISS MATTY, *her arms full of candles.*)

MISS MATTY	I'm sure there were more than this left – oh!
PETER	You must be the proprietor, ma'am.
MISS MATTY	Miss Jenkyns. You are, sir?
MAJOR ADAMS	Madam, don't say you do not know!
MISS MATTY	(*to* PETER) Should I recognise you, sir?
MAJOR ADAMS	I thought –
PETER	When we arrived in Cranford, you benevolently directed us to our lodgings.
MISS MATTY	A pleasure to meet you properly, Mr – ?
PETER	Major . . . Wick.

(MAJOR ADAMS *looks at* PETER *curiously.*)

MAJOR ADAMS	Major Adams.
MARY	Mrs Forrester said you have lately been in Bombay. Did you see any tigers?
MAJOR ADAMS	I confess I think I have met with more tigresses this week than I ever did in India. But in exchange for your name, I will transport you on a veritable safari.
MARY	Miss Mary Smith.
MISS POLE	(*to* MARY, *sotto*) Miss Smith, I hear safaris are most hazardous.

(MARY *sits with* MAJOR ADAMS. *They talk.*)

MISS MATTY	(*to* PETER) Tea then, sir.

PETER   I don't suppose you have coffee?

MISS POLE   In a teashop?

PETER   How foolish of me.

                (MISS MATTY *makes tea.*)

                What prompted you to open a tearoom as
                opposed to a coffeehouse, madam?

MISS MATTY   Tea is neither greasy nor sticky. Grease and
                stickiness are two qualities I simply cannot
                endure.

MISS POLE   You shall have to adjust that opinion. Babies
                are generally sticky and greasy in equal
                measure.

PETER   You mean – Miss Smith, should I have
                congratulated you?

MISS POLE   You shall not find any unmarried lady in
                Cranford in an expectant state!

                (MISS MATTY *pours the tea.*)

PETER   No milk, thank you.

MISS POLE   Nonsense.

                (MISS POLE *adds milk to his cup.*)

MISS MATTY   Mince pie?

                (MARY *takes a mince pie.*)

MISS POLE   What are you doing? It is most vulgar for a
                lady to partake of pastries with her tea when
                in company.

(MISS POLE *takes the mince pie from* MARY.)

PETER   A mince-pie-inflated waistline is of no
                use to a young woman hoping to ensnare a
                husband, is it, Miss Smith?

MISS POLE   She has no such thoughts!

                (*Enter* BETTY *with bottles.*)

BETTY   Miss Pole ma'am, I've brought round them
                lemonade dregs for yer party.

                (MISS POLE *tries to nod her head sideways at
                the men without being noticed.*)

                Why yer noddin' yer head like that, ma'am?
                Beggin' yer pardon, but I've gotta be quick,
                I'm in the middle of washin' yer delicates.

                (MISS POLE *jumps up to hurry* BETTY *away.
                Her cards scatter. She scrabbles to pick
                them up but* PETER *gets there first.*)

PETER   Your Christmas cards, madam.

MISS POLE   They are not Christmas cards! They are
                letters.

PETER   In such festive wrapping.

MISS POLE   It is all the store stocks at this time of year.
                Most tedious.

PETER   Perhaps I can help you distribute them. They
                must be intended for hand delivery as they
                bear no address. He reads an envelope. Mrs
                Jamieson, is it?

                (MISS POLE *snatches the cards.*)

MISS POLE   You, sir, represent everything that ever
             discouraged me from marrying a man.

             (MISS POLE *hurries to* BETTY.)

PETER   (*laughing*) I did not mean to offend your
             postal propriety, madam!

             (*Exeunt* MISS POLE *and* BETTY.)

MISS MATTY   It is uncourteous to chortle at another's
             embarrassment.

PETER   I did not mean to –

MISS MATTY   We may live very quietly, but you will find
             that no resident of Cranford shall remain
             silent in the face of an attack upon her
             friends. Perhaps it is time you returned to
             Bombay or Barcelona or wherever it was
             you came from. Your jests may be better
             received there.

MAJOR ADAMS Allow me to apologise –

MISS MATTY   There is no need, Major Adams. You have
             not offended.

PETER   I understand, madam. You have made things
             clear.

             (*Exit* PETER.)

MAJOR ADAMS Miss Smith, we shall meet again.

             (*Exit* MAJOR ADAMS.)

MISS MATTY   I have never spoken so directly before. He
             must learn the consequence of his words.
             Poor Miss Pole will not recover easily from

such humiliation. I do not usually dare to warn young people against matrimony, but instances like this remind me that marriage is a risk. You can never know for sure how people will turn out.

(MARY *starts to go.*)

Where are you going, dear?

MARY   I delivered my Christmas cards this morning. I fear if Miss Pole returns home to find a red envelope upon the mat then . . .

MISS MATTY   She keeps a spare door key in the vegetable patch. Fetch the bonnets!

(*Exeunt. Blackout.*)

Scene Two

Outside MISS MATTY *and* MISS POLE'S *houses.*

Enter CAROL SINGERS. *They sing. The window of* MISS MATTY'S *house opens and* MISS MATTY *and* MARY *appear. They listen happily. The window of* MISS POLE'S *house opens and she appears, disapproving. A* SINGER *goes to* MISS MATTY'S *house with the collection tin.* MISS MATTY *and* MARY *put some money in.*

MISS POLE   They will never go away now!

SINGER   For charity, ma'am?

MISS POLE   It is reprehensible to pose as charity cases when there are many more deserving individuals not to be found soliciting on the street. No one could believe you to be needy in *that* coat.

SINGER   We are collecting. For the Drumble
                  Charitable Home for Orphans.

MISS POLE   I have never heard of such an institution.
                  Kindly move along.

                  (MISS POLE *retreats inside and slams her*
                  window shut. MISS MATTY *puts more money*
                  in the collection tin, retreats and closes her
                  window. The SINGERS *move closer to* MISS
                  POLE'S *house and launch into another carol.*
                  The window of MISS POLE'S *house opens and*
                  she appears, glaring. The SINGERS *continue.*
                  MISS POLE *disappears inside. A moment*
                  later, she reappears, produces a bugle and
                  blows it loudly. The SINGERS *jump and stop*
                  abruptly. Satisfied, MISS POLE *starts to*
                  withdraw.)

SINGER   Miss Pole.

MISS POLE   How do you know my name?

SINGER   You've called on my mother Mrs Fitz-Adam
                  every Friday since I was seven. I regret
                  to tell you we are no longer available to
                  perform at the Cranford Christmas party.

MISS POLE   Excuse me?

SINGER   You shall undoubtedly be glad to be rid of us.

MISS POLE   You were hired to sing at the party?

SINGER   Thinking that we would be treated with
                  respect, yes! We are much in demand, you
                  know, and shall not hesitate to contact the
                  Drumble local authorities and inform them
                  that we are now at liberty to perform at their
                  Christmas Eve concert.

MISS POLE   Then you have saved me the inconvenience
                   of informing you that your services are no
                   longer required.

SINGER   Then you have precisely what you wanted.

MISS POLE   Precisely.

                   (*Exeunt* SINGERS.)

                   Miss Matty! Miss Matty!

                   (*The window of* MISS MATTY'S *opens and*
                   MISS MATTY *appears.*)

MISS MATTY   Is that your father's bugle?

MISS POLE   Whoever it was that booked that miscreant
                   band of carollers to perform at the
                   Christmas party is going to be very sorry
                   they have let us down. A double booking in
                   Drumble, apparently.

MISS MATTY   We don't have any carol singers? This is all
                   getting very out of hand. Mary!

                   (MISS MATTY *retreats inside and closes her
                   window.*)

MISS POLE   Miss Matty, wait, I have a plan!

                   (*Enter a* PENNY POST BOY.)

PENNY POST   Any letters ter post? Christmas cards ter
                   send?

                   (*He sees* MISS POLE.)

PENNY POST   Ma'am? –

MISS POLE   Don't even think about it!

                   (MISS POLE *retreats inside and slams her*
                   window. Exit PENNY POST BOY. *Blackout*.)

                          Scene Three

MISS MATTY'S *teashop / parlour.*

MARY *is decorating the room, singing a carol to herself.*
Enter MISS POLE *and* MISS MATTY, *unnoticed by* MARY.

MISS POLE   I shall purchase the new napkins but
                   everything else must be ordered from
                   Manchester.

                   (*They see and hear* MARY *and stop to listen*.)

MISS MATTY   She had lessons when she was a girl.

                   (*Exit* MISS POLE. MISS MATTY *goes to*
                   help MARY. *Enter* MARTHA, *carrying a*
                   stepladder.)

MISS MATTY   (*in horror*) Martha!

MARY   What are you doing?

MARTHA   Bringin' in a ladder.

MISS MATTY   But you can't – not in your state!

MARTHA   My state?

MARY   Your state of . . . dress! You could . . . catch
                   your hem and trip.

MARTHA   I'm used ter hard work, miss.

(MARTHA *steps onto the first rung of the ladder.*)

MISS MATTY & MARY	No!
MISS MATTY	Martha, you mustn't!
MARTHA	Mustn't what?
MARY	Decorate the tree!
MARTHA	But it's Christmas. The party. Folk'll be expectin' a tree.

(MARTHA *goes to take a step.*)

MISS MATTY	The steps! The steps are broken!
MARTHA	Jem were up on 'em just yesterday fixing that leaky tile on the shed, ma'am.

(MARTHA *goes to take a step.*)

MISS MATTY	I hear Thomas calling. Hadn't you better see what's wrong?
MISS POLE	(*off stage*) Miss Matty! Miss Matty!
MARTHA	I can only hear Miss Pole, ma'am.

(*Enter* MISS POLE *with armfuls of holly and mistletoe. As* MARY *and* MISS MATTY *turn to greet her,* MARTHA *climbs the ladder and starts decorating the tree.*)

MISS POLE	I have brought these to make a new wreath.
MARY	To distract yourself?

MISS POLE	I do not need distractions. I have entirely forgotten about that odious Major Wicked.
MISS MATTY	Thomas brought in some very pretty ivy yesterday. Picked it himself.

(*Exit* MISS MATTY. MISS POLE *notices* MARTHA *on the ladder.*)

MISS POLE	You should not be gallivanting about like that in your condition!
MARTHA	Condition?
MARY	Yes! Vertigo! A terrible affliction.
MISS POLE	Reckless girl.

(MISS POLE *wanders over to the fire.*)

It is very cold today. You should put more coal on the fire.

MARY	I'll ask Jem to bring some in.

(*Exit* MARY, *confused.* MISS POLE *checks that* MARTHA *is not looking, reaches into her purse and withdraws the Christmas cards. She throws them on the fire. Enter* MISS MATTY *and* MARY *with a basket of ivy.*)

MISS POLE	Our carolling deficiency is resolved. Mary, you have the most experience, you will lead.
MARY	Lead what?
MISS POLE	The Cranford choir!
MISS MATTY	Who are the Cranford choir?

MISS POLE   We are.

MISS MATTY   I – I have never sung outside of Sunday
                     mornings!

MISS POLE   It cannot be hard, the amount of people who
                     manage to do it. Everything is arranged.
                     Rehearsal on Wednesday, seven o'clock.
                     There's enough here to make a wreath for
                     the teashop as well.

                     (MISS POLE *busies herself with the ivy as*
                     MISS MATTY *and* MARY *take some holly to*
                     arrange around the room. MISS POLE *sits*
                     with her back to the audience. Enter JEM
                     with coal. He sees MARTHA.)

JEM   What yer doin'? Get down from there!

                     (JEM *tries to grab* MARTHA *and lift her down.*
                     She struggles.)

MARTHA   Jem! Get off!

JEM   Yer might have an accident! If yer fell –

MARTHA   Yer the only thing what's gonna make me
                     have an accident, yer great oaf!

                     (*She shoves* JEM *and he lets go, stumbling.*)

JEM   Martha!

                     (MISS POLE *shrieks, leaping to her feet and*
                     spinning around: her face and hands are
                     bright red. MARTHA, *startled, teeters on the*
                     ladder and falls, crying out. JEM *manages to*
                     catch her.)

MISS MATTY   Martha!

MARY   Miss Pole!

MISS POLE   My face!

              (MISS POLE *starts scratching at her face,*
              hands and arms. JEM *lifts* MARTHA *into his*
              arms.)

MARTHA   Put me down, I'm fine!

MISS MATTY   We must call the doctor!

MARTHA   (*to* JEM) Stop embarrassin' me! Miss Matty,
              really, yer don't need ter – I'm not hurt.

MARY   But what about the baby?

              (*Beat.*)

MARTHA   What baby?

MISS MATTY   Martha, we know.

MARTHA   (*to* JEM) Yer told her! Yer promised, yer
              great big liar!

JEM   I didn't say owt! She probably noticed the
              great big bump stickin' out yer middle!

MARTHA   Callin' me fat now, are yer?

              (JEM *angrily puts* MARTHA *down.*)

MISS MATTY   It wasn't Jem. We . . . deduced the situation.

MARTHA   I'm sorry, Miss Matty ma'am. Are yer awful
              angry with me?

MISS MATTY   The only thing I could be cross about would
              be your refusal to see the doctor.

MARTHA	But –
MISS MATTY	I could not forgive myself if anything happened and I had not insisted.
	(MARTHA *gives in.*)
JEM	So yer'll listen ter her – no offence, Miss Matty ma'am – but not me?
MARTHA	Nothing's ever good enough for yer, is it? I don't know why I put up with yer!
MISS POLE	Cease your whining, girl! Be thankful you are not injured. Miss Matty, do you think it's Scarlet Fever?
MISS MATTY	It couldn't have come on so suddenly.
MARY	It looks like an allergic reaction to me.
MISS POLE	I did not know *you* were a qualified medical practitioner.
MARY	Maybe there are some nettles tangled in the holly.
MISS POLE	I didn't go near the holly – only that!
	(JEM *comes over to look.*)
JEM	No wonder yer all red, ma'am. That there's poison ivy
MISS POLE	I have been poisoned!
	(MISS POLE *hyperventilates and swoons.* MARY *tries to calm her.*)

MARTHA   Look what yer've done now! Yer should've
                  noticed it were poison.

JEM   Now everything's my fault? Be too much ter
                  hope I s'pose that I ain't ter blame for that
                  and all?

                  (JEM *gestures at her stomach.*)

MARTHA   How can yer say that, shamin' me in front o'
                  everyone?

MISS MATTY   That is enough! Martha. You shall go
                  upstairs, lie down and wait for the doctor.

MARTHA   But –

MISS MATTY   I hope I am not a harsh mistress, but on this
                  occasion, I will assert my authority.

                  (*Exit* MARTHA, *crossly.*)

                  Jem, send Thomas to fetch Dr Hoggins.

                  (*Exit* JEM.)

                  Miss Pole, you are having an allergic
                  reaction. Your life is not in peril, but you
                  shall go upstairs with Mary and apply
                  calamine lotion to the inflamed area.

MISS POLE   What if there is . . . scarring?

MISS MATTY   There will not be, but Dr Hoggins can
                  confirm it.

MISS POLE   Must it be him?

MISS MATTY   I do not understand your quarrel with
                  him. He is accomplished and aside from

the ignominy of visiting women in their bedchambers, I cannot see why anyone would have a complaint against him.

MISS POLE   His name is coarse.

MISS MATTY   But if he changed it to Piggins it would not be much better. He is the only doctor within thirty miles as you well know. Make haste to the calamine.

(*Exeunt* MISS POLE *and* MARY. MISS MATTY *goes to pick up the ivy, stops and covers her hand with her apron. She throws it on the fire. She takes up her cameo.*)

I did not think a Christmas party could be the foundation of such friction. Of course, the addition of an expectant maid does not ease the predicament. I know you were never fond of children, but I find myself quite light-hearted at the thought of a little baby crawling about the place.

(*The doorbell rings.* MISS MATTY *puts her cameo away. Smoke begins to exude from the fireplace. Enter* LADY GLENMIRE.)

LADY GLENM.   (*with a Scottish accent*) Hello. Are you open for service?

MISS MATTY   I apologise, we are a little muddled this afternoon.

(*She shows* LADY GLENMIRE *to a seat.*)

LADY GLENM.   This is most homely. I have been in so many teashops where you can hardly sip your tea for fear of disrupting some sacrosanct oath of silence!

MISS MATTY   Company makes tea taste all the finer.

LADY GLENM.   What blends do you have?

MISS MATTY   A very agreeable Earl Grey . . . also a new
              Oolong, which I have yet to sample.

LADY GLENM.   How exotic! Shall we perhaps try some
              together?

              (MISS MATTY *takes the Oolong tea and starts
              making two cups.*)

MISS MATTY   Are you new to Cranford? Things are a
              little flustered with preparations for our
              Christmas Eve party. We have just formed a
              choir.

LADY GLENM.   Singing is such a joy.

MISS MATTY   Then allow me to invite you to join us.

LADY GLENM.   I would not want to intrude.

              (MISS MATTY *gives* LADY GLENMIRE *her cup
              of tea.*)

MISS MATTY   The more the merrier. Wednesday at seven.

              (*They drink. Enter* MARY *and* DR HOGGINS.)

DR HOGGINS   Plenty of rest. Nervous energy can severely
              unbalance the humours.

MISS MATTY   Martha is bedridden?

DR HOGGINS   No, she is fit as a fiddle. Miss Pole.

(*Enter* MISS POLE, *her face covered with thick white paste and her hands heavily bandaged.*)

MISS POLE   I am quite capable of being in company with Mary and Miss Matty.

(MISS POLE *sees* LADY GLENMIRE.)

LADY GLENM.   Good day!

MISS POLE   Good day.

(MISS POLE *struggles to pick up a newspaper, open it and hide behind it.*)

MISS MATTY   The baby is healthy?

DR HOGGINS   A fine, strong specimen. I wager she'll have a strapping young boy before St Valentine's!

MISS POLE   St Valentine's! It is strong, so it is undoubtedly a girl.

MISS MATTY   And the lotion?

DR HOGGINS   To calm the hives.

MISS POLE   Dr Hoggins, must you use that term? I have never had anything to do with bees.

DR HOGGINS   It will alleviate the inflammation. A recipe of my own invention. All natural ingredients.

LADY GLENM.   How clever.

DR HOGGINS   I have devised ointments to treat several unsightly skin ailments.

MISS POLE   Unsightly!

DR HOGGINS   But this is not a topic of conversation that
                 interests ladies. I ought to compliment the
                 furnishings or the comment on the weather.

LADY GLENM.   On the contrary, it is fascinating.

                 (DR HOGGINS *sits with* LADY GLENMIRE. *They
                 talk animatedly. Enter* JEM.)

JEM   Miss Matty ma'am?

                 (MISS MATTY *goes aside with* JEM.)

                 I just wanted ter say that if yer want us ter
                 leave, we'll understand and there'd be no
                 hard feelings like, none at all. We've been
                 right grateful for all yer've done for us.

MISS MATTY   Leave? You must not go anywhere! Unless
                 you wish to?

JEM   I speak for Martha too, ma'am, when I say
                 that nowt'd please us more than ter stay with
                 yer here. I'll do all I can ter make it easy on
                 yer, ma'am.

                 (*Exit* JEM. MISS MATTY *returns to the group.*)

MISS POLE   It is lewd and degenerate.

MARY   (*to* MISS MATTY) Dr Hoggins and Lady
                 Glenmire have just expressed a shared
                 admiration for country dancing.

MISS POLE   Is something burning?

MARY   Thomas hasn't put the wooden spoons in the
                 oven again? It does seem a little smoky.

(LADY GLENMIRE *breaks into a coughing fit.*)

DR HOGGINS   Water!

MISS MATTY   Tea?

(LADY GLENMIRE *drinks some tea.*)

DR HOGGINS   You haven't got a headache? A temperature?

(DR HOGGINS *tries to put his hand on* LADY GLENMIRE'S *head to see if she has a fever.*)

MISS POLE   Dr Hoggins! Reserve that behaviour for your private examinations!

(MARY *starts coughing.*)

Not you as well!

MARY   Miss Matty, the fire! They move aside, revealing smoke pouring out of the fireplace.

MISS POLE   Fire! Fire!

MARY   There aren't any flames.

(DR HOGGINS *leans over the fireplace to investigate.*)

MISS MATTY   Careful, doctor!

MISS POLE   Someone should fetch water in case. Fires can be impulsively explosive.

(*A sudden bang from the fire makes the ladies jump.*)

MISS POLE   You see!

MARY   Dr Hoggins?

MISS MATTY   Sir, are you well?

                (DR HOGGINS *turns around, revealing that
                his face has been completely blackened by
                soot.*)

MISS POLE   Dr Hoggins!

                (LADY GLENMIRE *begins to laugh.*)

LADY GLENM.   Forgive me!

                (MISS MATTY *and* MARY *cannot help but
                begin to laugh as well.*)

DR HOGGINS   Something is amusing?

                (MISS POLE *tries to cover her amusement
                with disapproval. Enter* MRS JAMIESON,
                unnoticed.)

                Do I have something on my face?

                (*They laugh louder.*)

MRS JAMIESON   (*in horror*) Lady Glenmire!

MISS POLE   Where?

                (*They turn and see* MRS JAMIESON. LADY
                GLENMIRE *jumps to her feet.*)

                Lady Glenmire?

MRS JAMIESON   It appears I am seeing in monochrome. Miss
                Pole. Dr Hoggins.

MARY   Mrs Jamieson, we did not know you would be calling today.

MRS JAMIESON   I did not intend to. Then I was inconvenienced to spend all afternoon hunting around the village for a misplaced houseguest.

LADY GLENM.   I did not realise these were your friends.

MRS JAMIESON   I think it's time to leave. I assume you are finished scampering about the village?

DR HOGGINS   Mrs Jamieson, I have something of interest to you.

MRS JAMIESON   I doubt that very much.

                    (DR HOGGINS *carefully picks a charred red envelope out of the fire.*)

DR HOGGINS   Addressed to you, madam. Hot off the press.

                    (DR HOGGINS *laughs at his joke.* MISS POLE *snatches the envelope.*)

MISS POLE   You are mistaken, Dr Hoggins. This is not for you at all, Mrs Jamieson.

                    (MISS POLE *drops the envelope with her bandaged hands.*)

MRS JAMIESON   Miss Pole, if you desire so ardently to give me a Christmas card, I advise you to put it in the post and be done with it!

                    (*Exit* MRS JAMIESON.)

LADY GLENM.   I am so grateful for your – for the tea. Let me find my purse –

MISS MATTY   It is the least we may offer a dear relative of
                Mrs Jamieson's.

LADY GLENM.   Good day, ladies. Doctor.

                (*Exit* LADY GLENMIRE.)

MISS MATTY   I had no idea it was she all along.

                (MISS POLE *is trying to rip up the envelope*.)

MISS POLE   Mr Johnson should make known the
                incendiary risk of the stationary supplies he
                stocks. I can't think how these came to be
                on the fire.

MISS MATTY   I think poison ivy is more likely to incite a
                smoking fire than Christmas cards.

MARY   You tried to burn it?

MISS POLE   The smoke could be noxious?

DR HOGGINS   Neither Christmas cards nor ivy have been
                touched by any flames, ladies. A blocked
                chimney is to blame. A bird's nest, I don't
                suppose. Or perhaps Saint Nick arriving
                early after one too many mince pies? You
                may rest easy, ladies.

MARY   Doctor, there is a mirror in the hall. You
                may wish to avail yourself of it.

                (*Exit* DR HOGGINS, *perplexed*.)

MISS POLE   Rest easy! How could we? I despise him
                quite as much as ever.

MARY   Saint Nick?

MISS POLE   Dr Hoggins! Why did he have to be here
             when Lady Glenmire called? I am very
             distressed to have been in the presence of
             a lady and to have not even known it. But
             what is worse – did you see her? A mere ten
             pounds would easily have purchased every
             stitch she had on – lace and all!

             (*Blackout.*)

Scene Four

Cranford Village Square.

Enter CAROL SINGERS. *They sing. Enter* MRS JAMIESON,
pursued by MR MULLINER *holding Peppo.*

MR MULLINER   My lady! My lady!

               (MRS JAMIESON *takes Peppo from* MR
               MULLINER. *Enter* LADY GLENMIRE.)

LADY GLENM.   Mrs Jamieson, wait!

MRS JAMIESON   Mulliner, the sedan. We are leaving town.

LADY GLENM.   Where are we going?

MRS JAMIESON   Peppo and I are going to Manchester. (*To the*
               SINGERS.) Abort that undignified yowling!

LADY GLENM.   Mrs Jamieson!

               (*Exeunt* MRS JAMIESON *with Peppo, followed
               by* MR MULLINER.)

               Mrs Jamieson, wait!

(*Exit* LADY GLENMIRE. *The* CAROL SINGERS
finish their carol triumphantly. Curtain.
End of Act Two.)

ACT THREE

Scene One

Outside MISS MATTY *and* MISS POLE'S *houses.*

Enter CAROL SINGERS. *They sing. Enter* JEM *with a wreath and carpenter's bag. He goes to* MISS POLE'S *house. The window of* MISS POLE'S *house opens and* MISS POLE *appears. She shows* JEM *where to hang the wreath and he starts working. She sees the* SINGERS *and shuts her window. The carol finishes. Exeunt* SINGERS. *Enter* PETER, *pursued by* MAJOR ADAMS.

PETER | It's been long enough.

MAJOR ADAMS | You didn't come all this way to give up, not even –

PETER | I will not dredge up the past. She doesn't recognise me.

MAJOR ADAMS | Why lie to her?

PETER | To spare her.

MAJOR ADAMS | Spare her what? Go and see her. Talk to her. You'll regret it if you don't. Peter, you know you will –

PETER | Don't say that name. Not here. Not in Cranford.

MAJOR ADAMS | Because you have transformed into Major Wick? Or because she might remember?

PETER | Because all the memories – the hope I once invested in that name are gone, perished with the past. There is nothing here for me.

It all happened too long ago. Miss Matilda
Jenkyns shall be left to her life – her quiet,
peaceful life.

(*Exit* PETER. *Exit* JEM, *having overheard
while putting up the wreath. Enter* MARY *in
cloak and bonnet.*)

MARY   Good day, Major Adams.

MAJOR ADAMS   Where are you hurrying off to?

MARY   Mr Johnson catches the train to Manchester
              this afternoon and must be charged with
              purchasing everything for the Christmas
              party. Woe betide him if he returns without
              the crackers.

MAJOR ADAMS   Then I must ensure you arrive safely to
              place your order.

MARY   You want to avoid someone.

MAJOR ADAMS   You speak plainly.

MARY   Your companion? There is discord between
              you?

MAJOR ADAMS   Our apologies will no doubt be lubricated by
              the cherry brandy Mrs Forrester serves after
              dinner. May I ask you something?

MARY   You can certainly ask.

MAJOR ADAMS   Does Miss Jenkyns ever talk about the past?

MARY   She has been known to ponder on the Civil
              War, Henry VIII, 1066 . . .

MAJOR ADAMS   You are teasing me.

MARY   Perhaps *you* should speak more plainly.

MAJOR ADAMS   A gentleman from the past.

MARY   Shakespeare or Dr Johnson?

MAJOR ADAMS   Of close acquaintance.

MARY   I cannot answer that.

MAJOR ADAMS   A question too far.

MARY   I can't answer because I don't know. She
                gives no hint of any gentlemen at all to me.

MAJOR ADAMS   What made you confide in me?

MARY   I suppose I trust you. Speaking plainly.

MAJOR ADAMS   There is little *plain* about supposing it.
                Thank you, Miss Smith.

MARY   Mary.

MAJOR ADAMS   Miss Mary Smith.

MARY   Try it without the Miss and lose the Smith.

MAJOR ADAMS   Surely that would be most improper in the
                middle of a public highway?

MARY   People frequently indulge in many improper
                things when no one is watching.

MAJOR ADAMS   Even in Cranford?

MARY   Only when the train to Manchester is not
                waiting to be missed, Major Adams.

MAJOR ADAMS   Edward.

MARY   *That* would be very improper.

                (*Exeunt* MARY *and* MAJOR ADAMS. *Blackout.*)

                            Scene 2

Cranford Village Square.

MISS POLE, MISS MATTY, MARY, BETTY *and* DR HOGGINS *are
assembling for choir practice.* MISS POLE *hands out song
sheets.*

BETTY   (*to* MISS POLE) Why did I have ter come?
                It's freezin' out here. Yer could've had Mrs
                Forrester if yer'd let her.

MISS POLE   We will have no deaf choristers on my
                watch. Carol singers have to be immune to
                inclement temperatures. You best get used to
                it. (*To* MARY.) You must command attention
                if you're going to conduct.

MARY   Conduct?

                (MISS POLE *pushes* MARY *forward.*)

                Let's start with the first verse, then.

                (MARY *counts them in. They sing.* DR
                HOGGINS *drowns everyone out but has a
                good voice.*)

                You have a very strong voice, doctor.

BETTY   That's a polite way o' sayin' yer sing too
                loud, sir.

MISS POLE   (*to* BETTY) We do not need a running
                commentary.

DR HOGGINS   (*to* BETTY) Are you sure it's not that you sing too softly?

MISS POLE   Refrain from speaking to my maid in that manner, sir! That is just the sort of comment commonly made by a m–

DR HOGGINS   A man?

MISS POLE   A medical professional. No wonder there are so many sneezes and sniffles in the village. Instead of tending the sick, you have been tuning your vocal chords. I knew this was all a very bad idea from the start.

(MISS POLE *starts to go. Enter* LADY GLENMIRE *and* MR MULLINER.)

Your Ladyship!

LADY GLENM.   Are you leaving? Am I too late? Or perhaps you have all the carollers you need.

MISS MATTY   You are exactly on time.

(LADY GLENMIRE *joins* MISS MATTY. MISS POLE *hurries over to* MARY.)

MISS POLE   What should we talk to Her Ladyship about?

MARY   Weren't you discussing flannel petticoats when we met her last week?

MISS POLE   I didn't know who she was then! What is a suitable topic to discuss with a member of the peerage?

LADY GLENM.   Mr Mulliner, come and sing. You will enjoy it.

MR MULLINER   Delightful, my lady.

(MR MULLINER *reluctantly joins the group.*
BETTY *spies him with interest. During the*
following, she tries to edge nearer to him.)

MISS POLE   (*to* LADY GLENMIRE) I should so like to know
                   how the queen is. Has Your Ladyship been
                   to court lately?

LADY GLENM.   Never in my life! I've only been to London
                   once.

MARY   I'd love to go to London.

LADY GLENM.   Perhaps one day we might all go together!

MISS POLE   Oh, Your Ladyship!

                   (BETTY *bumps into* MISS POLE *while trying to*
                   get near MR MULLINER.)

                   What are you doing, girl?

BETTY   Trying ter get warm, ma'am.

MISS POLE   Do it in a more stationary manner.

MARY   Let's look at the next verse.

MISS POLE   As long as we are not overpowered by
                   boisterous braying this time.

LADY GLENM.   Braying?

MISS POLE   Dr Hoggins took it upon himself to
                   impersonate a depraved donkey.

LADY GLENM.   You are out of practice, doctor? I am
                   competent on the pianoforte – perhaps we
                   could rehearse together?

| DR HOGGINS | Private tuition? |

| MARY | The doctor is being very modest. |

| DR HOGGINS | The truth is that I cannot sing at all. |

| LADY GLENM. | I am sure someone else would be a much more proficient teacher than I, but I would be delighted to attempt some lessons. |

| DR HOGGINS | It wouldn't be a burden? |

| LADY GLENM. | Let us fix upon a time. |

(BETTY *bumps into* MISS POLE *as she heads for* MR MULLINER.)

| MISS POLE | The last time I looked, you were not a frog. Stop this absurd bouncing about. |

| BETTY | It were a shiver. |

| MISS POLE | Then control your bodily functions. |

| MARY | Let's sing in rounds for now. Ladies take the first verse, gentlemen the next, then everyone for the chorus. So, ladies – |

(MARY *counts the* WOMEN *in and sings with them. Enter* MAJOR ADAMS. *He watches until the verse finishes then applauds.*)

| MAJOR ADAMS | Bravo, Miss Mary Smith. |

| MARY | You persist in your strategy of avoidance then. |

| MAJOR ADAMS | I was merely out walking when I was disturbed by some near deafening caterwauling. |

MARY   Yet you stopped to listen.

MAJOR ADAMS   No, I stumbled over here to escape the
                catfight that disrupted my walk. Singing in
                the street must surely be a highly improper
                activity.

MARY   Only if you object to frozen lips and the
                chattering of teeth.

MAJOR ADAMS   As long as the teeth are in tune.

MARY   And what of the lips?

                (*A commotion as* BETTY *fakes a swoon,
                throwing herself at* MR MULLINER.)

MISS POLE   Betty!

                (MR MULLINER *lowers* BETTY *to the ground.
                Everyone gathers around.*)

                Get up this instant!

MR MULLINER   Madam, she is cold.

MISS POLE   She's not dead!

                (DR HOGGINS *crouches by* BETTY.)

DR HOGGINS   Betty? Can you hear me?

BETTY   Where am I? Where am I?

DR HOGGINS   How do you feel?

BETTY   It ain't hypothermia, doctor?

DR HOGGINS   No. But let's get you into the warm.

(MR MULLINER *and* DR HOGGINS *help*
BETTY *to her feet. She leans heavily on* MR
MULLINER.)

MISS MATTY	My house is nearest.
MARY	She can't go alone. The burglars!
MISS POLE	(*to* LADY GLENMIRE) We have everything here in Cranford. London has very little that we don't.
BETTY	Now yer mention it, I'd be mighty glad o' someone – a man ter protect me on me way.

(MAJOR ADAMS *steps forwards.*)

Mr Mulliner'll take me, won't yer?

MISS POLE	Mr Mulliner is here to wait on Lady Glenmire.
LADY GLENM.	No, please, we must get her into the warm!

(*Exeunt* MR MULLINER *and* BETTY.)

MAJOR ADAMS	I thought this was a rehearsal.
MARY	It is.
MAJOR ADAMS	*That* was quite a performance.
MARY	You have learnt to speak plainly at last.
MAJOR ADAMS	I was taught by the best, Miss Mary Plain.
MARY	You can join us. If you want to.
MAJOR ADAMS	I have some business to attend to.

MARY   Business.

MAJOR ADAMS   Christmas cards do not write themselves, you
                know. Meet me. The day after tomorrow.

MARY   On Christmas Eve?

MAJOR ADAMS   Here. Four o'clock.

MARY   And outside calling hours?

MAJOR ADAMS   I didn't think you were afraid of offending
                propriety.

MARY   I am not. Edward.

MAJOR ADAMS   Then I shall leave you to continue these
                degenerate exploits.

                (*Exit* MAJOR ADAMS.)

MISS POLE   Miss Smith, do you intend to make an ice
                sculpture of us?

MARY   Gentlemen . . . Dr Hoggins. Your verse.

LADY GLENM.   Must the poor man fend for himself?

                (DR HOGGINS *sings, remembers he is
                not supposed to be able to, and wavers
                ridiculously.*)

                It is worse than I thought. I think the doctor
                and I will be spending a lot of time together.

                (*The* WOMEN *join in the chorus. Blackout.*)

Scene Three

MISS MATTY'S *teashop / parlour.*

Evening. The room and Christmas tree are fully decorated.
Crashes and bangs from offstage. Enter MR MULLINER *and*
BETTY, *wrapped around each other. They stumble, bumping*
into things. BETTY *tears herself away and tries to compose*
herself. She casually glances at MR MULLINER, *but looks*
away when he looks. Beat. They leap on each other, falling
to the floor behind the sofa.

MISS POLE	(*off stage*) Betty? Betty!

(BETTY'S *head pops up behind the sofa,*
wearing MR MULLINER'S *wig.*)

(*off stage*) Betty!

(BETTY *disappears behind the sofa, then*
emerges. Her cap is missing. MR MULLINER
emerges, adjusting his wig. BETTY *looks for*
somewhere to hide him, then shoves him
back behind the sofa. Enter MISS POLE, MISS
MATTY, MARY *and* LADY GLENMIRE *removing*
their cloaks and bonnets.)

LADY GLENM.	I don't know how they could steal so close to Christmas.
MISS POLE	Thieves have no respect for the season of goodwill.
LADY GLENM.	(*to* BETTY) How are you now?
BETTY	Better, ma'am.
MISS POLE	Your Ladyship, Betty! You look different.

(BETTY *realises her cap is missing and tries to look for it without being noticed.*)

MARY   Where's Martha?

BETTY   Gone ter bed, miss. Yer know ma'am, yer should have a word with her. Tell her ter go easy on the mince pies.

MISS POLE   Go and put the kettle on!

                  (*Exit* BETTY, *glancing back nervously at the sofa.*)

LADY GLENM.   Is she well enough?

MISS POLE   Tea is a great restorative. The fact that they are troubling themselves with trifling items is what's so very worrying. Sponge fingers. Baubles.

MARY   Christmas wreaths.

MISS POLE   We must implement security measures.

MISS MATTY   Is that really necessary?

MISS POLE   Just because you are fortunate enough to live in a very creaky house, we cannot all rely on a squeaking floorboard to alert us to an intrusion! There must be no opportunity to gain entry to our homes. Every caller must submit to questioning. To verify they are who they say they are.

MARY   I don't think burglars knock before they come in. Even in Cranford.

LADY GLENM.   With my accent, you will not doubt it is I coming to call!

MISS POLE   Accents merely increase the risk of
                 impersonation. But close acquaintances such
                 as Your Ladyship do require an alternative
                 method of identification.

LADY GLENM.   What wonderful friends Mrs Jamieson has.

MISS POLE   There is nothing else for it. We shall have to
                 employ the secret signal.

MARY   The what?

                 (MISS POLE *prepares to demonstrate her
                 knock on the table.* MR MULLINER *sneezes.*)

LADY GLENM.   Was that a creaking floorboard?

                 (*Enter* BETTY *with the tea tray.*)

MARY   It sounded like a sneeze.

MISS MATTY   It came from near the ground.

MISS POLE   Ladies, I have prepared for this moment.

MARY   What moment?

MISS POLE   Fear not. I shall investigate.

BETTY   Investigate what?

MARY   A sneeze.

MISS POLE   A burglar!

BETTY   That were me.

                 (MR MULLINER'S *boots are visible.* BETTY
                 *kicks them and they disappear. She fakes a
                 sneeze.*)

Told yer I'd catch cold singin' outside.

MISS MATTY   We are getting far too suspicious. Would you bring the biscuits, Betty? Cupboard over the sink.

(*Exit* BETTY.)

MISS POLE   One can never be too guarded. I keep a rolling pin under my pillow.

MISS MATTY   Ever since I was a girl, I have dreaded being caught by the leg while getting into bed by someone concealed beneath. I used to leap into bed and bring both my legs up at once. I am more graceful nowadays of course, but the terror has come upon me often since these attacks began.

MARY   A peek under the bed should calm your fears?

MISS MATTY   It is too unpleasant to think of looking and seeing a man hidden there. I keep my hand near the bell, ready to call out to Jem so an intruder might know there is a man in the house.

MISS POLE   They are useful for some things.

LADY GLENM.   Bells?

MISS POLE   Men.

MARY   I have an idea.

(MARY *takes a bauble off the Christmas tree.*)

MISS POLE   To vandalise the Christmas tree?

MARY   Every night, take something round and roll
              it under the bed. When it appears the other
              side you can rest easy.

              (MARY *rolls the bauble under the sofa. The*
              WOMEN *wait for it to reappear.*)

LADY GLENM.   Perhaps it's caught in a crack in the
              floorboards.

MISS POLE   Is your house built on an incline?

              (MARY *rolls another bauble under the sofa.*
              They wait.)

              Miss Matty. Remain calm. I knew it. There
              is a robber under your sofa.

MARY   There can't be.

MISS MATTY   How could he have got there?

MARY   There must be another explanation –

LADY GLENM.   I think there *is* someone under the sofa.

MARY   Why?

LADY GLENM.   I can see his boots.

              (MR MULLINER'S *boots are visible. They*
              withdraw quickly. MISS POLE *goes to the*
              fireplace and takes the poker.)

MISS POLE   After three, lift the throw. One.

              (MARY *takes hold of the throw.*)

              Two.

(MISS POLE *poises with the poker.*)

Three.

(*Enter* BETTY, *her mouth full.*)

BETTY   There weren't no biscuits left, ma'am –

(*They try to shush* BETTY.)

BETTY   What yer doin'? Miss Pole, ma'am, yer
           shouldn't be brandishin' that about!

(BETTY *tries to take the poker.*)

MISS POLE There's a burglar under the sofa.

BETTY   Ma'am, yer havin' one o' yer funny turns
           again –

(MISS POLE *regains her hold on the poker.*)

MISS MATTY Mary, call for Jem –

BETTY   There's no need, ma'am, there's nowt under
           sofa, I'll check for yer –

(*The* WOMEN *stop her.* MR MULLINER *sneezes.*
MISS POLE *starts towards the sofa.* BETTY
leaps at MISS POLE *and tries to manhandle
the poker from her.*)

MISS POLE She's lost her mind! Help me!

BETTY   Yer'll do yerself a mischief, ma'am!

MISS POLE I'll do *you* a mischief! Give me that!

(BETTY *seizes the poker but stumbles
backwards, tripping and falling onto the*

sofa just as MR MULLINER *pops up behind it,
holding up* BETTY'S *cap. The* WOMEN *shriek
in surprise.*)

MISS MATTY   Mr Mulliner!

MARY   What are you doing?

BETTY   Lookin' for my cap!

MR MULLINER   Found it, madam.

                  (BETTY *snatches the cap.*)

MISS POLE   (*to* BETTY) You knew it was him under there?

MARY   Why didn't you just say?

BETTY   I thought yer'd be cross I'd lost me cap.

MISS POLE   It is very foolish to sneak about when there
                  are burglars on the loose.

BETTY   He didn't mean ter scare yer, ma'am –

MISS POLE   I was not afraid. (*To* MR MULLINER.) I have
                  never been more thankful Mrs Jamieson
                  went away! As if she has not already been
                  disgraced enough.

MISS MATTY   Betty, would you check we haven't disturbed
                  Martha?

                  (*Exit* BETTY.)

LADY GLENM.   Perhaps we should be on our way, Mr
                  Mulliner. May we walk you home, Miss
                  Pole?

MISS POLE   I shall remain here tonight. Miss Matty and
                 Mary would not want to be alone after such
                 an ordeal. (*To* MISS MATTY.) You two can
                 share, can't you?

LADY GLENM.   Mr Mulliner. Quickly. Quickly.

                 (*Exeunt* LADY GLENMIRE *and* MR MULLINER.)

MARY   Mr Mulliner really hasn't been the same
                 since Mrs Jamieson left. He must miss her
                 terribly.

MISS MATTY   (*to* MISS POLE) I am glad you didn't lose your
                 temper with Betty. She was quite frantic for
                 her lost cap. Poor girl.

MISS POLE   Poor girl nothing! Betty! Betty!

                 (*Exit* MISS POLE.)

MARY   Miss Pole! You'll wake Martha!

                 (*Exit* MARY. MISS MATTY *replaces the poker
                 by the fire. She removes her cameo and puts
                 it in a trinket box. As she goes to leave, she
                 glances at the tree. She takes a bauble and
                 rolls it under the sofa. It emerges. She picks
                 it up, satisfied. Exit* MISS MATTY. *Blackout*.)

Scene Four

MISS MATTY'S *teashop / parlour.*

LADY GLENMIRE'S *mouth is full of sweets.* MISS POLE *is
standing, her dress covered with brooches.*

MISS POLE   Repeat after me, Your Ladyship. Miss
                   Marchland and Miss Madison and Mrs
                   Molly May –

                   (LADY GLENMIRE *repeats. It is unintelligible.*)

                   A couple more, I think.

                   (MISS POLE *inserts more boiled sweets into*
                   LADY GLENMIRE'S *mouth. Enter* MARY *and*
                   MISS MATTY *with Christmas stockings.*)

MISS MATTY   (*to* MARY) Did you bring the pins, dear?

                   (*They see* LADY GLENMIRE.)

MARY   What are you doing?

MISS POLE   Curing Her Ladyship of her accent.
                   Impersonation prevention.

MARY   You're wearing seven brooches.

MISS POLE   Don't you know it's rude to count a lady's
                   accessories?

MISS MATTY   Those aren't marbles in Lady Glenmire's
                   mouth?

MISS POLE   Of course not. That would be highly
                   dangerous. She could choke. They're boiled
                   sweets. After me, Your Ladyship. Doctor
                   Dawkins, Doctor Dunlop, Doctor Drake and
                   Doctor Drill –

MARY   Is this safe?

MISS POLE   I would not enact a procedure on Her
                   Ladyship without having first undertaken

the necessary research. I read about it in my
magazine.

(*Enter* THOMAS, *covered in flour.*)

THOMAS　　　Miss Matty ma'am!

MISS POLE　　You.

THOMAS　　　Ma'am?

MISS POLE　　Be in no doubt, boy, that I am highly trained
in deadly nightshade detection.

MISS MATTY　Thomas didn't know it was poison ivy.

MISS POLE　　Not a drop of arsenic will get past me.

MARY　　　　Arsenic?

MISS POLE　　Reeks of garlic. I am always particularly
suspicious of the French.

THOMAS　　　Miss Matty ma'am, it's the mince pies.

MISS MATTY　I thought Martha left instructions?

THOMAS　　　But she didn't leave the meat.

MISS MATTY　The meat has already been minced and
mixed with fruit.

THOMAS　　　Fruit? So it's sweet?

MISS POLE　　You sound like you've never had a mince
pie.

THOMAS　　　I ain't, ma'am.

MISS MATTY	Cupboard next to the oven for the jar of mincemeat. One spoonful in each pie.

(*Exit* THOMAS.)

MISS POLE	Doctor Dawkins, Doctor Dunlop –

(LADY GLENMIRE *tries to repeat but is even more illegible.*)

MARY	I'm not sure it's working.

(MISS POLE *picks up the sweets.*)

MISS POLE	One more, Your Ladyship –

(MARY *intervenes.*)

MISS MATTY	Elocution lessons must be very taxing. I'm sure you both need a break.

MARY	How is Lady Glenmire to expel the sweets?

(*Enter* MRS JAMIESON *and Peppo, unnoticed. She watches.*)

MISS MATTY	Quickly, a bowl.

MISS POLE	We cannot do it in here! What if someone were to see? To come in? It's the middle of calling hours.

(*Unnoticed by the others*, LADY GLENMIRE *spits the sweets out.*)

MISS MATTY	We cannot leave Lady Glenmire stranded in this state.

LADY GLENM.	Ladies, please –

MISS POLE   Your Ladyship, do not trouble yourself –
                   Mary, go and –

                   (*Beat. The* WOMEN *turn to look at* LADY
                   GLENMIRE *in horror.*)

MARY   You didn't swallow them?

LADY GLENM.   No! I spat them out.

                   (MISS POLE *goes to sit down, then leans on
                   the table instead.*)

MRS JAMIESON   I see nothing has changed during my
                   absence.

LADY GLENM.   Mrs Jamieson?

MISS MATTY   We did not expect you – we did not know
                   you had returned to Cranford.

MRS JAMIESON   The city grew tiresome. So many people,
                   such hustle and bustle. Poor Peppo did not
                   like it one bit, did you my little poochiewoo?
                   I hope I shall not regret returning so soon.

LADY GLENM.   I'm sorry, Mrs Jamieson –

MRS JAMIESON   I assume tea is on its way.

                   (MISS MATTY *starts to get up but* MARY *stops
                   her. Exit* MARY.)

                   It is that tiresome doctor I still have quarrel
                   with. You have not seen him since the
                   fireplace fiasco.

MISS POLE   Hardly at all.

MRS JAMIESON   I hope he is suitably ashamed of himself.

(*Enter* MARY *and* DR HOGGINS.)

MARY   Look who I found hanging up his coat in the hall!

DR HOGGINS   Mrs Jamieson, returned! What a happy day!

MRS JAMIESON   It is?

MISS POLE   Don't you have an expectant patient?

DR HOGGINS   Almost seven months.

MISS POLE   That is not what I meant –

DR HOGGINS   I have indeed come to see Martha.

LADY GLENM.   Have some tea first.

MARY   Fresh mince pies are on their way.

MRS JAMIESON   How terribly festive.

MARY   Everything is, here. We have even started a choir.

MRS JAMIESON   Precisely what does that entail?

LADY GLENM.   Carolling.

MRS JAMIESON   Not outside?

LADY GLENM.   Al fresco is all the fashion.

MRS JAMIESON   You don't mean in the streets?

MISS POLE   It is very pleasant to see the stars.

MRS JAMIESON   You are doing it at night?

DR HOGGINS   Astronomy is a fascinating science.

MISS POLE   It is the trade of swindlers and crooks. Just
                  last week my horoscope instructed me to
                  manage a misunderstanding with calm and
                  poise. Ludicrous.

MRS JAMIESON   You are confusing astronomy with astrology.
                  Perhaps that was your misunderstanding.

MARY   It sounds like sage advice.

MISS POLE   I expect it was written by a man. Predicting
                  things is just their sort of game. They have
                  a habit of telling you after a disaster has
                  occurred that they foresaw it coming. My
                  father was a man, so I know the sex pretty
                  well. But I cannot be calm when there are
                  robbers on the rampage.

MRS JAMIESON   They are not still at large?

MISS POLE   It has been necessary to implement
                  measures to ensure our safety.

MARY   A secret knock.

LADY GLENM.   It is very clandestine.

MRS JAMIESON   (*to* LADY GLENMIRE) You are sanctioning
                  these frivolities?

DR HOGGINS   Lady Glenmire has been kept quite safe.

LADY GLENM.   We are neutralising my voice. Accents
                  complicate identification. So troublesome.

DR HOGGINS   Troublesome? It is part of you. Do not desire
                  to change a thing.

MRS JAMIESON   Rapping on doors is a vain enterprise. A
                house is much more likely to be attacked
                when it is silent and empty.

MISS POLE   This is just what I have come to realise.

                (MISS POLE *removes her shawl and starts to
                pull her skirt up.*)

MRS JAMIESON   Peppo is not accustomed to such depravity!
                Peppo, avert your eyes!

MARY   She is only revealing the ankle.

MRS JAMIESON   The most provocative part!

MISS POLE   Any burglar attacking my house while I am
                out will not find anything of worth there. I
                carry all my treasures on my person.

MARY   That explains the brooches.

                (MISS POLE *reveals silverware and cutlery
                strapped to her ankles and arms.*)

MRS JAMIESON   You are a target for a direct assault.

MISS POLE   I do not advertise my goods. They are
                hidden in concealed places. I read the queen
                always wears her brooches like this.

MRS JAMIESON   I suggest you put your hoard away before it
                is observed by would-be muggers.

                (MISS POLE *drops her skirt and pulls her
                shawl on.*)

                Sit down before I suffer altitude sickness
                from looking up at you. I am quite
                lightheaded.

MISS POLE   I cannot.

MRS JAMIESON   Cannot what?

MISS POLE   Sit down.

MRS JAMIESON   Why not?

MISS POLE   My gilt serving spoon.

MARY   Dr Hoggins! Have you seen Mr Dickens'
                 Christmas Carol?

MRS JAMIESON   Not that ghastly thing. I cannot understand
                 the fuss.

LADY GLENM.   Have you read it?

MRS JAMIESON   Ghosts? At this time of year?

MARY   It receives high acclaim.

MRS JAMIESON   Perhaps if the author perseveres very
                 hard, he might one day make something of
                 himself.

                 (*Enter* THOMAS *with a tray of tea and mince
                 pies.*)

THOMAS   Mince pies, hot from the oven!

MRS JAMIESON   Your teashop is rowdier than the Manchester
                 market, Miss Matty.

                 (*The* WOMEN *and* DR HOGGINS *all take a
                 mince pie.*)

THOMAS   I spent all mornin' on the pastry, ma'am.
                 Put my hands on an icicle ter get em proper
                 cold.

MRS JAMIESON	I hope it was a clean icicle.

(They take a bite. They chew, pleasantly surprised, then freeze, mid-chew. MISS MATTY swallows with effort.)

THOMAS	Did I do summit wrong?
MISS MATTY	What recipe did you use?
THOMAS	Just like yer told me, spoonful from the jar.
MISS MATTY	Bring me the jar you used.

(Exit THOMAS, confused. MISS POLE, MRS JAMIESON, MARY and LADY GLENMIRE grab serviettes and spit out their mouthfuls. DR HOGGINS swallows.)

MISS POLE	What has he done to them?
MRS JAMIESON	Surely mince pies are not hard to get right?

(Enter THOMAS with a jar. MISS MATTY takes it.)

MISS MATTY	This is the jar you used?
MISS POLE	He's poisoned me again, hasn't he?
THOMAS	It says meat on it!
MISS MATTY	But not mincemeat.
MRS JAMIESON	I know I will regret asking this, but what does it say?
MISS MATTY	Sweetmeats.

(The WOMEN react with horror.)

THOMAS   Ma'am, yer said it's sweet! Sweet meat!

MISS MATTY   Sweetmeat is something quite different.

THOMAS   Bad different?

MARY   It's the term for a certain part of the animal.
                Not usually spoken of in teashops.

MRS JAMIESON   Peppo, no! Peppo is tucking into the pies.
                Leave those nasty things alone! Peppo!

LADY GLENM.   I feel a little queasy. Excuse me –

                (*Exeunt* LADY GLENMIRE *pursued by* DR
                HOGGINS.)

THOMAS   Miss?

                (MARY *whispers in* THOMAS' *ear.*)

                Miss Matty! I wouldn't have thought yer'd
                have summit like that in yer kitchen!

                (THOMAS *snatches the pies and jar. Exit*
                THOMAS.)

MRS JAMIESON   My doubts about returning to Cranford so
                soon were woefully justified. I hope you are
                pleased with yourselves. You have goaded
                my poor helpless Peppo into cannibalism.
                Shame on you all. No progress has been
                made whatsoever. I hope you all have a very
                jolly Christmas party together tomorrow!

                (*Exeunt* MRS JAMIESON *and Peppo.*)

MISS POLE   Just when I thought things couldn't get any
                worse!

(MISS POLE *goes to throw herself into a seat.*)

MARY   Miss Pole!

MISS MATTY   The spoon!

(MISS MATTY *and* MARY *rush to catch* MISS POLE *before she sits. Blackout. End of Act Three.*)

ACT FOUR

Scene One

Cranford Village Square.

Enter CHESTNUT SELLER, *cooking chestnuts on a brazier.*
Enter MARY, *fastening her bonnet. The* SELLER *indicates to*
the chestnuts, but MARY *declines. She pulls a sprig of holly*
out of her purse, fiddles with it. She wanders back and
forth before calming herself. She waits. Fade to spotlight on
MARY.

Scene Two

MISS MATTY'S *teashop / parlour.*

MISS MATTY *is knitting.*

MISS MATTY   I don't suppose we shall see Mrs Jamieson
               until the New Year now, Deborah dear.
               I confess, I am not sure I am quite as
               regretful about that as I should be.

               (*Enter* JEM.)

MISS MATTY   Is it Martha – ?

JEM   She's eatin' her pork pie and custard. I
               wanted ter talk ter yer, Miss Matty ma'am.
               There's summit what I need ter tell yer.

MISS MATTY   Jem, I knew this time would come. I respect
               whatever decision you and Martha have
               made.

JEM   Martha? This ain't got nowt ter do with her.

MISS MATTY   You haven't come to tell me you're leaving?

JEM   We're right settled here, ma'am. Unless yer
               want us out from under yer feet –

               (MISS MATTY *stops him.*)

               It's about them two gentlemen lately come
               ter Cranford. I'd never willingly interfere
               with no man's business and I've been in two
               minds bout tellin' yer, but I heard Major
               Wick say yer name in amongst talk o' the
               past. Seemin' like he knows yer ma'am or
               thinks he does.

MISS MATTY   Major Wick?

JEM   'Cept he ain't all he says he is. Accordin' ter
               his friend, his name's Peter.

MISS MATTY   Peter?

JEM   It means summit ter yer?

MISS MATTY   No. No, it doesn't.

JEM   Then I'm sorry I troubled yer. I just felt it
               were me duty ter tell yer. 'Cos if yer knew
               who he was and he weren't a good sort, yer'd
               only have ter say the word and I'd see him
               straight out o' the village.

MISS MATTY   Thank you, Jem. You're very kind.

JEM   Reckon peace and quiet for yer sewing's the
               best kindness I can offer yer, ma'am.

               (*Exit* JEM.)

MISS MATTY   Knitting.

(MISS MATTY *slowly goes to the fireplace.*
She hangs up two stockings. She picks up a
third stocking, holds it for a long moment.
She braces herself on the fireplace. Enter
PETER, *unseen. He sees* MISS MATTY, *takes*
a step towards her, stops and picks up the
hand bell. He rings it. MISS MATTY *turns,*
but freezes when she sees PETER.)

PETER   I startled you.

MISS MATTY   I didn't expect to see you again, sir.

PETER   After I offended I didn't expect you would
                 have to.

MISS MATTY   It is forgotten.

PETER   I was on course to leave Cranford. The last
                 train before Christmas. Preparations for the
                 party are going well?

MISS MATTY   You do not seem like the kind of man who
                 commonly engages in small talk, sir.

PETER   Am I so transparent? But you are right.
                 There is something I must say that can wait
                 no longer.

                 (*He takes a step towards* MISS MATTY. *She*
                 steps back.)

MISS MATTY   If you require tea, I can be of assistance.
                 But if not . . .

PETER   Matilda –

MISS MATTY   We are too recently acquainted for such
                 familiarity.

PETER   *Reacquainted.*

MISS MATTY   I do not like riddles, or tricks or ploys.

PETER   The truth. There is no Major Wick. There is
                  only me. Peter.

                  (*He steps towards* MISS MATTY.)

                  I realise this is a shock, but I can explain to
                  you –

MISS MATTY   I do not know where you learnt that name.

PETER   Learnt it? I think I know it pretty well,
                  being born with it.

MISS MATTY   The man who *was* born with it has died with
                  it as well.

PETER   You don't understand – of course, how could
                  you –

MISS MATTY   It is you who does not understand. Peter is
                  dead.

PETER   No, that was never true –

MISS MATTY   How you came to know of me, I cannot
                  imagine. You seek to exploit me perhaps.
                  I assure you I have no money whatsoever
                  and very little else. Your journey has been
                  wasted.

PETER   I came to talk to you. As a man to a woman.
                  Please allow me that chance –

MISS MATTY   You have come to my home, offended
                  my friends, and now insult me further by
                  speaking of the past – a past that does not

concern you. A past that I have put far
behind me. I wish you well but you shall
remain to me as much of a stranger as you
are today. Good day, sir.

(*She turns her back on* PETER. *He starts
towards her then stops himself and turns
on his heel. Exit* PETER. MISS MATTY *picks
up the stocking. She slowly sits, holding the
stocking tightly. Fade to spotlight on* MISS
MATTY.)

Scene Three

Cranford Village Square.

MARY *waits, weary, frozen. Enter* VILLAGERS. *They buy
chestnuts.*

VILLAGER	(*to* MARY) Merry Christmas, Miss!
MARY	(*flatly*) Merry Christmas.
	(*Exeunt* VILLAGERS, *laughing and chatting. The* CHESTNUT SELLER *packs up and starts to leave. Enter* MISS POLE. *She stops the* SELLER *to buy a bag of chestnuts. Exit* SELLER.)
MISS POLE	What are you doing out here, hanging about like an iceberg?
MARY	He said four o'clock.
MISS POLE	You are wallowing over a man? Stop immediately; I shall not allow it. Have a chestnut.
	(MARY *takes a chestnut, eats it.*)

MISS POLE   I shall give you some advice. A lady must be tardy to engagements involving a man. Any sign of enthusiasm makes them bolt like a pony. I expect he came along at ten past four, saw you waiting like a little lost kitten and turned directly on his heel. And you should not have waited so long. You cannot expect him to respect you if you have so little regard for yourself.

(MARY *sobs and runs off, dropping her holly. Exit* MARY.)

Miss Smith! Crying hinders digestion!

(*Exit* MISS POLE.)

Scene Four

MISS MATTY'S *teashop / parlour.*

MISS MATTY *holds the stocking. Enter* MARY, *fumbling to undo her bonnet and cloak.*

MISS MATTY   Mary? Here, let me.

(MISS MATTY *does it for her.*)

You're frozen.

(MISS MATTY *directs* MARY *to the fire and wraps her in a blanket.*)

MARY   He didn't come. Why didn't I know he wouldn't come?

MISS MATTY   Trust is a gift.

MARY   Or a burden. I have been . . . imprudent.

MISS MATTY   No one could find fault with anything you
              have done.

MARY   Miss Pole is right.

MISS MATTY   Miss Pole?

MARY   I knew I was letting my feelings control me
              – move me to ignore logic, reason.

MISS MATTY   We have all been guilty of that.

MARY   You are calm. Controlled. You cope.

MISS MATTY   Are your feelings for Major Adams strong?

MARY   They are new. Different.

MISS MATTY   Mary, Major Wick has left Cranford.

MARY   Major Adams has gone with him then. I
              cannot come to the party. It doesn't feel like
              Christmas at all.

MISS MATTY   I have done wrong by you, Mary. Major
              Wick left under my instruction.

MARY   He offended you further?

MISS MATTY   He came to see me, told me something –
              something I know to be untrue. He claimed
              to be someone. From the past.

MARY   Major Adams once asked me about your
              past.

MISS MATTY   What did you say?

MARY   I told him the truth. That I know nothing.

MISS MATTY	I have been unfair to you. I have accepted your friendship and offered so very little in return.
MARY	You don't have to share everything to be the dearest friend I've ever known.
MISS MATTY	When I was younger, there was someone who meant very, very much to me. Someone who has not been in my life for a long time.
MARY	A man.
MISS MATTY	Yes. But not as you think. He was –

(*Enter* MISS POLE *carrying a boxed Christmas present.*)

MISS POLE	Aren't you two getting ready for the party? I found this on your front step. It looks highly suspicious.
MISS MATTY	A present.
MISS POLE	A wolf in festive wrapping. It might have been left by a burglar. It could be an incendiary device.
MARY	I don't think demolition is a burglar's intent.
MISS POLE	We should inspect it further.

(MISS MATTY *opens the box.*)

Don't blame me when a robber leaps out.

MARY	Of that?
MISS POLE	Contortionists have a very unlawful look about them.

(*She and* MARY *try to peer into the box.* MISS
MATTY *freezes.*)

MARY   What is it?

(MISS MATTY *slowly withdraws a jar of
marmalade.*)

MISS POLE   Marmalade? Is there a note? If it's from Mrs
Forrester, don't eat it. She gave me lemon
curd with whole lemons in, rind and all.
Who knows what she does to her oranges.

MISS MATTY   It's from Peter.

MISS POLE   We do not know any Peters.

MISS MATTY   *Peter* Peter.

(MISS POLE *is shocked.*)

MISS POLE   Matty, are you well? Is it the cold?

MISS MATTY   He's returned. He's in Cranford!

MISS POLE   Matty, you remember what happened?

MISS MATTY   I can't believe it.

MISS POLE   You have done too much – too many
preparations for the party.

MISS MATTY   I turned him away.

MARY   Who?

MISS MATTY   Peter. My brother.

MISS POLE   Matty, Peter is dead.

(MISS MATTY *goes to her trinket box and rifles through until she finds a letter.*)

(*to* MARY) Quickly, the doctor. She's not well. I have never seen her like this.

MISS MATTY   I do not need the doctor. Mary, many years ago I received this letter, informing me that my brother, Major Peter Jenkyns, had been killed in service in the East Indes. This afternoon, Major Wick came to see me. To tell me he is my brother.

MISS POLE   You did not believe him!

MISS MATTY   Not then. But I do now. He has proved beyond doubt that my brother is alive – that he is my brother. When Peter was small, he was once asked his name. Instead of saying Peter Marmaduke as he meant to, he mistakenly said Peter Marmalade. From that moment on, my sister and I secretly called him Marmalade. No other soul has ever known before now. I must get to the station before the train leaves. She puts the letter in the box. Mary, have you seen my cameo?

MARY   You were wearing it the other day.

MISS MATTY   I put it in here. It's gone!

(*The sound of a shot being fired.*)

MISS POLE   Someone has been shot!

(MISS MATTY *and* MARY *get up.*)

What are you doing? There is a gunwielding madman, an armed robber, the ringleader of a murderous gang running about the village!

MARY   What if someone's hurt?

MISS MATTY   We'll stay close together, and return at any
                sign of danger.

MISS POLE   If we are taken hostage, it shall not be my
                fault.

                (*Exeunt. Blackout. End of Act Four.*)

ACT FIVE

Scene One

Cranford Village Square.

Enter MISS POLE, MISS MATTY *and* MARY *nervously. Enter a disguised* BURGLAR, *clutching flowers. He barrels past, almost knocking* MISS POLE *over. Exit* BURGLAR.

MISS POLE   Don't fuss over me – that was the thief! After him!

                   (*Enter* DR HOGGINS *in pursuit.*)

DR HOGGINS   Stop there! Thief!

                   (*Exit* DR HOGGINS. *The sound of another gunshot. Enter* MRS JAMIESON, *holding Peppo, pursued by* LADY GLENMIRE.)

LADY GLENM.   Mrs Jamieson!

MRS JAMIESON   I have nothing to say to you.

MISS POLE   Mrs Jamieson, be wary! There is a burglar.

MRS JAMIESON   You think I don't know? He has just attempted to break into my house. I set Mulliner onto him with Mr Jamieson's musket. We would all be dead if it weren't for my brave, clever boy.

MARY   Mr Mulliner?

MRS JAMIESON   Peppo! He was dozing in his window side cot when he spied the villain scrabbling about in the flowerbeds and courageously raised the alarm.

LADY GLENM.   As soon as he heard Peppo yapping, Dr
               Hoggins went after the robber.

MISS POLE   What was he doing at your house?

MISS MATTY   Is someone ill?

MRS JAMIESON   Yes. Lady Glenmire has lost her senses. She
               was entertaining him at the pianoforte. It is
               depraved.

LADY GLENM.   I was teaching him. To sing.

MRS JAMIESON   Treachery!

LADY GLENM.   It's the truth.

MRS JAMIESON   Then how is it that Dr Hoggins used to be a
               chorister? It grieves me to say that for such an
               objectionable man, he did have a fine voice.

LADY GLENM.   Dr Hoggins can already sing?

MISS POLE   This was all a scheme to insinuate the wolf
               into the fold so he might steal away with the
               shepherdess.

LADY GLENM.   He never really needed lessons?

               (*Enter* DR HOGGINS *with the* BURGLAR.)

MRS JAMIESON   Dr Hoggins, will you stay away from my
               burglar!

               (*They see the* BURGLAR *is* THOMAS.)

MARY   It's Thomas, not the burglar!

THOMAS   Miss Matty ma'am –

MISS MATTY	Doctor, let go of him, he's distraught.

(DR HOGGINS *lets go of* THOMAS.)

Let's get you inside.

THOMAS	Stop, Miss Matty!

(*They look at him in shock.*)

It were me. I'm the thief.

MARY	You tried to break into Mrs Jamieson's?
THOMAS	No, miss.
MISS MATTY	Then what? –
THOMAS	I only wanted some flowers. For yer. Ter say sorry for the mince pies.

(THOMAS *holds the flowers out to* MISS MATTY. MRS JAMIESON *snatches them. The sound of another gunshot.*)

MRS JAMIESON	Somebody inform Mulliner the culprit has been apprehended before he makes Mrs Forresters of us all.

(*Exit* LADY GLENMIRE.)

DR HOGGINS	Lady Glenmire, let me accompany you –
MRS JAMIESON	Desist pestering my sister-in-law!
MISS POLE	To think you were harbouring the scoundrel within your very home, Miss Matty.

(*Enter* JEM, *running with his bag.*)

MARY   Jem? Where are you going?

JEM   Ain't yer heard bout the accident?

MISS MATTY   An accident?

JEM   Johnson's cart, comin' back from station,
                turned over on road. Horse were spooked by
                gunshots and swerved cart into ice on side
                o' the road.

MISS POLE   But the crackers!

MISS MATTY   Is anyone hurt?

MISS POLE   That's what I meant.

JEM   I don't know – all the lads are goin' ter help.

DR HOGGINS   I'll follow on.

JEM   Thomas? Comin'?

MISS POLE   He most certainly is not!

                (*Exit* JEM.)

MRS JAMIESON   Now the constable will be indisposed. How
                inconvenient.

MISS POLE   We are quite able to perpetrate our own
                justice.

MISS MATTY   Thomas, I want you to tell me honestly –
                truthfully – if you are responsible for the
                thefts.

THOMAS   I'm sorry, Miss Matty ma'am.

MISS POLE   His anguish bespeaks guilt.

MISS MATTY   Thomas?

                (THOMAS *slowly takes the cameo out of his pocket and holds it out.* MISS MATTY *takes it.*)

THOMAS   I never meant ter hurt yer, ma'am.

MRS JAMIESON   Remove him.

MISS POLE   We need a makeshift cell.

THOMAS   Miss Matty!

MISS POLE   Don't cry for your mistress now!

MISS MATTY   Take him to the shop.

MRS JAMIESON   It is insecure.

MISS POLE   Martha shall be a vigilant gaoler.

THOMAS   Miss Matty ma'am, I'm sorry! Miss Matty!

                (*Exeunt* DR HOGGINS *and* THOMAS.)

MRS JAMIESON   Come, Peppo. I promised I would reward his bravery with clotted cream. I shall return to pronounce my sentence.

                (*Exit* MRS JAMIESON *with Peppo.*)

MISS POLE   To think we thought poisoning the worst of his crimes.

MISS MATTY   I never thought an employee of mine would steal.

MARY   Let's find Mrs Johnson. Sit with her a while.

MISS MATTY   Yes. Some tea, perhaps. I suppose it is too
                  late now.

MISS POLE   Too late?

MISS MATTY   The train will have left. With Major Adams
                  upon it too. I am so sorry, Mary. So very
                  sorry.

                  (*Exit* MISS MATTY.)

MARY   Miss Pole, we have to find Peter. He must
                  come back. Miss Matty can't lose her
                  brother again.

MISS POLE   The last we heard of him before his death
                  was that he had been elected the Great Lama
                  of Tibet.

MARY   Tibet.

MISS POLE   There must be contact details for Tibet
                  somewhere. We'll check the directory.

                  (*Exeunt. Blackout.*)

                       Scene Two

MISS MATTY's *teashop / parlour.*

THOMAS *sits.* MARTHA *is on the floor painting words onto a
white sheet in red paint, glancing suspiciously at* THOMAS.
*She reaches to put the paintbrush in the paint pot and grabs
her stomach, wincing.* THOMAS *jumps up to help her.*

MARTHA   Stay where yer are, don't even try it!

                  (THOMAS *sits.* MARTHA *paints.*)

THOMAS   I'm sorry, Martha miss.

                (*Beat.* MARTHA *ignores him.*)

MARTHA   How could yer steal off Miss Matty? After
                all she's done for yer? No – no, I don't
                wanna hear yer excuses. Yer know I vouched
                for yer? Jem weren't happy bout yer comin'
                ter work here, not happy at all, but I gave
                yer character and promised yer'd serve Miss
                Matty well. Yer've let everyone down.

                (THOMAS *hangs his head.* MARTHA *paints,
                then grabs her stomach.*)

THOMAS   Is it the baby?

MARTHA   Mind yer own.

                (MARTHA *continues painting.*)

THOMAS   Am I gonna go ter prison?

MARTHA   Should've worried bout that before. Why
                d'yer do it? What made yer think –

THOMAS   'Cos I thought I'd get away with it. 'Cos I'm
                bad, ain't I? Bad bad bad.

MARTHA   Are yer? Are yer really?

                (THOMAS *meets* MARTHA'S *eyes. He is about
                to say something when she grabs her belly,
                cries out.* THOMAS *runs to her, knocking the
                paint tin over onto the sheet.*)

                Thomas, what yer –

THOMAS   I ain't gonna just sit and leave yer!

MARTHA   The paint, yer clumsy clod!

                (THOMAS *sees the spilt paint and puts the tin
                on the table.*)

THOMAS   Is it – are yer – is the baby all right?

MARTHA   Yer need ter get Jem.

THOMAS   I can't.

MARTHA   Yer won't get in no more trouble.

THOMAS   It ain't that – I'd go even if I were gonna
                get sent straight ter the workhouse! – but
                everyone's gone – gone ter help with the
                accident.

MARTHA   There must be someone!

                (*Beat.* THOMAS *takes* MARTHA'S *arm.*)

                What yer doin'?

THOMAS   We've gotta get upstairs.

                (*He helps* MARTHA *up.*)

                I think yer've sat in summit wet.

MARTHA   My waters've broken! It's comin' – the
                baby's comin'! It's too early!

THOMAS   We're gonna go upstairs then I'm gonna get
                the doctor – I'll run all the way –

MARTHA   There ain't time, Thomas.

THOMAS   Yer can't do this by yerself!

MARTHA   Stuff yer mouth! I ain't scared. Anyway, I
                ain't by meself.

                (*Exeunt. Beat. Enter* MISS POLE, MARY *and*
                MISS MATTY.)

MISS POLE   Your punishment awaits. Mrs Jamieson
                expects her flowerbeds to be spotless and
                that is just the start –

MARY   Where is he?

MISS POLE   I knew a teashop could not contain a
                hardened criminal. He has run away.

MISS MATTY   I thought I had taught him to face up to his
                responsibilities.

MISS POLE   You are not to blame. At least you are
                fortunate enough to have had your stolen
                goods returned. Who knows where in the
                world my wreath is?

MISS MATTY   What are we going to do? We'll have to
                cancel the party.

                (Enter THOMAS, *his sleeves rolled up and
                carrying a pail.*)

MISS POLE   Caught in the act!

                (MISS POLE *tries to take the pail, but* THOMAS
                won't let go.)

THOMAS   Miss Pole ma'am, I need it!

MISS POLE   Give it to me!

MARTHA   (*off stage, in pain*) Thomas!

MISS MATTY   Martha?

                (THOMAS *pulls the pail out of* MISS POLE's
                grasp. Exit THOMAS.)

MISS POLE   Barricade the doors; don't let him escape!

MARY   Miss Matty!

                (MARY *holds up the red sheet.*)

MISS POLE   There has been a murder! A murder in your
                house, Miss Matty! During calling hours!

                (*The sound of a baby's cry.*)

MISS MATTY   It can't be.

MISS POLE   Not another catfight. This neighbourhood is
                going to wrack and ruin.

MARY   Martha!

                (*Enter* THOMAS.)

THOMAS   Miss Matty ma'am! She's had it! Martha's
                had her baby!

                (MISS MATTY, MISS POLE *and* MARY *exclaim
                in shock and delight.*)

MARY   What is it?

THOMAS   A baby, miss, I told yer.

MISS MATTY   Is she all right? Thomas, is she well?

THOMAS   She says she's bloomin' marvellous, ma'am!

                (*Exit* THOMAS. *Enter* PETER, *unnoticed.*)

MISS MATTY   A baby, a real kicking, giggling –

MISS POLE   – screeching –

MISS MATTY   – baby!

PETER   I seem to be in the habit of intruding.

                (*The* WOMEN *turn to see* PETER. MARY *pulls*
                MISS POLE *back as* MISS MATTY *and* PETER
                regard each other. PETER *slowly steps*
                forward, extends a hand.)

                Miss Matilda Jenkyns. I should be honoured
                to make your acquaintance. If it would
                please you to know me better.

                (*Beat.*)

MISS MATTY   You must mean re-acquaintance. Peter
                Marmalade Jenkyns.

                (MISS MATTY *all but runs into his arms.*
                MARY *starts to cry.*)

MISS POLE   Spare us your sentimental sniffles, girl.

                (MISS POLE *brushes at a tear.* MARY *pulls at*
                a reluctant MISS POLE. *Exeunt* MISS POLE *and*
                MARY.)

MISS MATTY   You came back.

PETER   Your mysterious marmalade merchant. No
                more tricks now. I am an open book.

MISS MATTY   No one can wholly be an open book. But I
                would be grateful for all you might share.

                (*Enter* THOMAS. *He retreats.*)

Thomas. For what you have done to help
Martha, I will be always grateful.

THOMAS   I'm so very sorry, Miss Matty. I never meant
ter do such terrible things. I only thought ter
help my mam.

MISS MATTY   Your mother? Why does she need help?

THOMAS   She ain't well, ma'am. Can't work or nothin'.
Not now. I just – I took the sponge fingers
and baubles and the wreath ter cheer her up
like. I never meant owt bad by it. But I know
it were wrong. The flowers really were for
yer.

MISS MATTY   And my cameo?

                (THOMAS *turns away.*)

                The brave do not run, Thomas.

                (*Beat. He turns back.*)

THOMAS   I were gonna sell it. She needs medicine. A
doctor. I were always gonna get it back for
yer, make it up ter yer somehow.

MISS MATTY   We shall see she gets the best care.

THOMAS   I don't deserve no help, ma'am.

MISS MATTY   I shall decide that. All I ask is that you
speak to me if you ever have a problem
again.

THOMAS   Yer mean I can stay? What bout the other
ladies, ma'am, they're awful cross –

MISS MATTY   We will explain to them together.

PETER	Man's capacity for forgiveness is a remarkable thing.
MISS MATTY	And woman's even more so. It fills the heart with a warmth that is not easy to forget.
THOMAS	I think I know it already, ma'am.

(THOMAS *turns, then looks back*.)

Thank yer, ma'am.

(*Exit* THOMAS.)

PETER	What a woman Miss Matilda Jenkyns is.
MISS MATTY	One who forgets too easily. I doubted you.
PETER	I don't think I come across as a very desirable brother.
MISS MATTY	You are the only brother I ever want.

(*Enter* MISS POLE *and* MARY.)

MARY	Miss Matty, you must go and see for yourself. Once you forget the initial horror of being in the birthing chamber, it is quite wonderful, really!
MISS MATTY	I will. (*To* PETER.) But I must know how you are here. Why you're not on the train to Manchester.
MISS POLE	And then Tibet.
PETER	Tibet? I stood on the platform, and I realised that if my gift had done as it intended, given you the proof you needed, I couldn't

abandon the chance to see you again. To
meet with you as myself. As your brother.

MISS MATTY   And Major Adams?

PETER   We parted at the station. I don't know if he
                got on. He has been so influential in all of
                this. We met in Burma. Not Tibet.

MISS POLE   It's all the neighbourhood of India.

PETER   When you received word of my death, I had
                in fact been taken prisoner. My regiment
                didn't know where I was.

MARY   They assumed you had died in battle.

PETER   I met Major Adams during my imprisonment
                and when we were released, he urged me to
                return here with the letter from my regiment
                revoking my death. It is possible to be
                reborn after all.

MISS POLE   (to MARY) That sounds like something the
                Lama would say.

                (PETER shows them the letter.)

MARY   Why didn't you give Miss Matty this
                immediately? It proves everything.

PETER   I suppose I wanted to be recognised. For
                who I am.

MISS MATTY   I failed you.

PETER   Never. If the marmalade hadn't done it, then
                maybe . . . You did not expect a family for
                Christmas.

MISS MATTY	I did not expect the family I have around me to *grow* this Christmas.

(*Enter* JEM, *laden with bags.*)

JEM	Miss Matty, I've got yer shoppin' from Johnson.
MISS POLE	Thank heavens the crackers are saved!
MARY	Is everybody all right?
MISS POLE	That's what I meant.
JEM	Doctor strapped up Johnson's leg but it ain't broke.

(JEM *sees the red sheet.*)

	There ain't been an accident here?
MARY	Not exactly.
JEM	Someone's hurt?
MISS POLE	Calm yourself.
JEM	I ain't gonna be calm when there's blood all over and my Martha's the only one not here.
MISS MATTY	It is Martha –
JEM	What happened?
MARY	She had some pains –
JEM	What kinda pains?
MISS POLE	Baby pains.

MARY   The baby started to come –

JEM   She ain't due for another two months! It's
                too early – too dangerous –

MISS MATTY   Jem, there's something you must understand,
                something – you are a – that is to say you
                are –

JEM   Don't! Don't say it, Miss Matty!

                (JEM *sinks to the floor, clutching the red
                sheet.*)

MISS POLE   What is he doing?

MARY   He must be overcome with the joy.

                (*Enter* MARTHA *in a nightgown with a bundle
                in her arms, unnoticed.* JEM's *shoulders are
                shaking.*)

MISS POLE   He doesn't look very joyful.

MARTHA   What yer blubberin' for yer great oaf?

                (JEM *looks up in shock.*)

                Ain't yer gonna come and say hello ter yer
                daughter then?

                (JEM *sweeps* MARTHA *into his arms.*)

JEM   I thought yer were dead! I saw the sheet –

MARTHA   Covered in red paint, yer fool.

JEM   Paint?

MISS POLE   We told you you were a father. I don't think we could have been much clearer.

MARTHA   This donkey 'ere just wanted an excuse ter wet his eyes.

JEM   Don't need no excuse. They kiss.

MISS MATTY   Now I can give you this. She holds up a knitted babysuit.

MARTHA   It's beautiful. Thank yer, ma'am.

MISS MATTY   *She* is beautiful.

(*Exeunt* JEM *and* MARTHA. *Enter* MAJOR ADAMS, *unnoticed.* MISS POLE *sniffs, sobs.*)

MARY   Is that a tear I see in your eye?

MISS POLE   I don't know how you can be so stonyfaced!

MARY   Let's find you a handkerchief.

(MARY *guides* MISS POLE *away but sees* MAJOR ADAMS *and* freezes. *Exit* MISS POLE.)

MAJOR ADAMS   You look like you've seen a ghost.

MARY   You're supposed to be on a train.

MAJOR ADAMS   I was supposed to meet you today.

MARY   You are not very good at keeping your word.

MAJOR ADAMS   It goes hand-in-hand with not speaking plainly. I am in need of more tuition.

MARY   Is that all you need?

MAJOR ADAMS   I wanted to – to – give you your Christmas
               card.

               (MAJOR ADAMS *holds out a Christmas card.*
               MARY *slowly reaches out and takes it.*)

MARY   You certainly do require more instruction in
               plain speaking.

MAJOR ADAMS   What should I have said?

MARY   That you came back for – for the party.

MAJOR ADAMS   *That* was plain, was it? I could not miss
               Cranford at Christmas. Or the party.

MISS MATTY   The party! Nothing's ready!

PETER   Let's start by putting the kettle on. Have you
               bought any coffee yet?

               (*Exeunt* MISS MATTY *and* PETER.)

MAJOR ADAMS   You look extraordinarily . . . plain.

MARY   You shall need to learn faster than that.
               Edward.

               (*Exeunt.*)

Scene Three

MISS MATTY's *teashop / parlour.*

PETER *and* MAJOR ADAMS *hang up a "Happy Christmas
Cranford" banner. Enter* MISS MATTY, MISS POLE *and* MARY
carrying plates laden with food including a huge turkey.

MARY	Miss Matty. Thank you. You showed me it is not a weakness to trust again.
MISS MATTY	Mary, you may never know how much my faith in the world has been revived by you.
MISS POLE	What are you two whispering about?
MARY	Charity.
MISS POLE	I have been thinking about that myself. I think I shall donate some money to the Drumble Charitable Institution. They should not suffer just because they are associated with a band of rogue carollers.

(*Enter* DR HOGGINS *with* LADY GLENMIRE, MR MULLINER *and* MRS JAMIESON *holding Peppo.*)

MISS MATTY	I am proud to introduce my brother, Major Peter Jenkyns.
MRS JAMIESON	A brother? Where have you been hiding him all these years?
PETER	Tibet.
MRS JAMIESON	What were you doing there? I don't know why anyone ever goes to Derbyshire.
PETER	I'm sure I could convert you to its charm.
MRS JAMIESON	You think so, do you?
DR HOGGINS	Excuse me, everyone. I have a question that I need to ask someone.

(*He goes on one knee in front of* LADY GLENMIRE *and* MRS JAMIESON.)

I can wait no longer. I must ask if I may have this lady's hand in marriage, Mrs Jamieson.

MRS JAMIESON   I do not wish to marry you at all!

DR HOGGINS   I would like your blessing to marry Lady Glenmire. She has given her consent.

MISS POLE   During one of their seditious singing sessions, I suppose. I have always thought teaching is a very scandalous profession.

LADY GLENM.   I know we have our differences, but I hope you might be happy for us.

PETER   An admirable union. Don't you think, Mrs Jamieson?

MRS JAMIESON   Arise, doctor.

(*She offers him an envelope.*)

DR HOGGINS   A Christmas card. For me.

MRS JAMIESON   You will join us for Christmas dinner.

DR HOGGINS   I would be delighted.

(DR HOGGINS *kisses* LADY GLENMIRE.)

MRS JAMIESON   It is churlish to maintain a grudge, don't you think Major Jenkyns? One must not stand in the way of young – mature love.

PETER   Quite so. Congratulations!

ALL   Congratulations!

(LADY GLENMIRE *reveals her ring.*)

PETER   Feast your mince pies on that, ladies!

DR HOGGINS   She is marrying me for my surgery, I am
                 sure of it.

LADY GLENM.   I always dreamed of my own stethoscope!

MRS JAMIESON   You do not need to divulge your dark desires
                 to us.

MISS POLE   One does not know whose turn may come
                 next. Here in Cranford poor Lady Glenmire
                 might have thought herself safe.

MISS MATTY   She does not seem too distressed.

                 (MISS POLE *pulls out a card.*)

MISS POLE   I hope you will accept this, Mrs Jamieson.

MRS JAMIESON   Thank you. I am a firm advocate of moving
                 with the times, you know, Major.

                 (*She sees* MAJOR ADAMS *holding mistletoe
                 over* MARY'S *head.*)

                 And yet we do not need to move quite
                 so quickly, Miss Smith! Why must
                 gentlemen keep a constant supply of that
                 cankerblossom in their top pockets at this
                 time of year?

PETER   I cannot imagine.

                 (MARY *kisses* MAJOR ADAMS. *Peppo starts
                 nestling at* PETER.)

MRS JAMIESON   Major, he likes you! How . . . promising.

(MISS MATTY *and* MISS POLE *hand out
crackers. Everyone forms a semicircle and
crosses arms.*)

MISS MATTY   My dear, dear friends. It warms my heart
                to share this party and all the delights of
                Cranford at Christmas with you. My brother
                – how wonderful it is to say that! – my
                brother and I wish you all a very merry
                Christmas!

ALL   Merry Christmas!

                (*They pull the crackers and dance in a
                circle.*)

MARY   Look! It's starting to snow!

                (*They all rush to look. Exeunt.*)

Scene Four

Cranford Village Square.

It is snowing. Enter MISS POLE, MISS MATTY, PETER, MARY,
MAJOR ADAMS, DR HOGGINS, LADY GLENMIRE, MR MULLINER
and MRS JAMIESON *with Peppo. They marvel at the snow.*
MAJOR ADAMS *sweeps* MARY *into a dance, followed by* LADY
GLENMIRE *and* DR HOGGINS *then finally* PETER *and* MISS
MATTY. *The others watch. As the dancing finishes, they
gather together to form a choir and sing. Curtain.*